STRASBOURG

TRAVEL GUIDE 2025-2026

Discover the Magic of Alsace – From France Historic Landmarks and Scenic Views to Cozy Cafes, Vibrant Markets, and Secret Spots Only Locals Know"

ALL RIGHTS RESERVED

DISCLAIMER

The information provided in *Strasbourg Travel Guide 2025–2026* is intended for general informational purposes only. While every effort has been made to ensure the accuracy and reliability of the content at the time of writing, travel-related details such as transportation schedules, admission fees, business hours, visa requirements, and other services may change without notice. Readers are encouraged to verify all current information with official sources, local authorities, or service providers before making travel arrangements.

This guide is based on publicly available information, independent research, and subjective interpretation. The author and publisher do not assume any responsibility or liability for any loss, damage, injury, or inconvenience sustained by any person using this guide. All travel is undertaken at the reader's own risk.

References to specific businesses, accommodations, or attractions do not imply endorsement. Likewise, the absence of any such references does not indicate disapproval. The inclusion of websites, contact details, or addresses is for convenience only and does not guarantee continued accuracy or service availability.

This publication is not affiliated with or endorsed by any government agency, tourism board, or trademarked entity in France or abroad. All trademarks, service marks, and logos mentioned herein are the property of their respective owners.

By using this guide, the reader agrees to hold the author and publisher harmless from any outcomes arising from the use of the information provided.

TABLE OF CONTENT

Chapter 1: Introduction to Strasbourg

1.1 Overview of Strasbourg

Strasbourg isn't the kind of place you just stumble into. It's a city you arrive in with a plan—or at least a sense of curiosity. Sitting right on the border between France and Germany, Strasbourg is where two worlds meet and shake hands. It's French, sure—but listen long enough and you'll hear the lilt of German in the architecture, the food, the street names, even the rhythms of everyday life. It's this cultural tug-of-war that gives Strasbourg its depth—and makes it one of the most int

eresting cities in Europe to explore.

Strasbourg is the capital of the Grand Est region of France and also the official seat of the European Parliament. That alone sets it apart—it's one of only a few cities in the world to host major international institutions without being a national capital. But don't let the political title fool you: Strasbourg is as intimate and walkable as a storybook village, despite its global importance. Cobbled lanes, half-timbered houses, flower-filled balconies, and riverside cafés give the city a charm that feels as if it's been carefully preserved through centuries of history—and in many ways, it has.

A City With Layers

Strasbourg is old. Really old. Founded by the Romans as Argentoratum over 2,000 years ago, it has weathered wars, revolutions, annexations, and peace treaties—all while managing to hang on to its identity. In the Middle Ages, it became an important hub of trade and learning. By the 17th century, it was a city that sparked ideas and movements, from humanism to printing. Later, it would be passed back and forth between France and Germany like a well-worn book—so much so that locals often describe themselves as Alsatian first, French or German second.

Today, the historical core of Strasbourg—known as the Grande Île—is a UNESCO World Heritage Site. That designation isn't just a label; it's a testament to how well Strasbourg has preserved its historic fabric. The medieval cathedral rises from the heart of the city like a stone flame. Narrow streets coil around Renaissance buildings and canals curve through quarters that haven't changed much since the 1500s. But just a few blocks over, you're suddenly in a sleek, modern district filled with glass-and-steel EU buildings and contemporary art.

Strasbourg blends eras like most cities blend neighborhoods. You don't have to go far to find contrasts: Catholic and Protestant churches stand within shouting distance of each other; a Gothic cathedral overlooks a tram station built last year. You'll walk past a museum showcasing 18th-century paintings, then turn a corner and see students gathered at a startup hub. It's all connected. And that's part of what makes Strasbourg so alive—it's living history.

Culture at the Crossroads

Being at the crossroads of France and Germany does something to a city's personality. It softens borders and encourages complexity. Strasbourg is fluent in both French and German traditions, but it doesn't lean too hard into either. That's where Alsatian culture comes in—its own dialect, its own food, its own way of doing things. Walk into a winstub (a traditional Alsatian tavern) and you'll see what I mean. The menu will have choucroute garnie (sauerkraut with sausages and meats), tarte flambée (a kind of crispy flatbread), and flan à la cannelle (cinnamon custard), all served with local wines from the nearby Alsace vineyards.

Then there are the festivals—Strasbourg doesn't take its celebrations lightly. The city's Christmas market, for instance, is one of the oldest and largest in Europe. It transforms the historic center into a glowing maze of lights, wooden stalls, and warm mulled wine. But it's not just about holidays. Strasbourg hosts a rich calendar of music, film, and cultural festivals year-round, drawing crowds from across Europe and beyond.

An Ecological and Forward-Looking City

Strasbourg is also one of the greenest cities in France—not just in trees and parks, though there are plenty—but in philosophy. It's known for its dedication to cycling, sustainable living, and innovative urban planning. The city's tram network is clean, efficient, and beautifully integrated into its surroundings. Bike lanes are everywhere, and there's a growing emphasis on walkability. Local authorities take pride in balancing historic preservation with a modern, eco-conscious mindset.

Strasbourg also leads in education and research. Home to the University of Strasbourg, one of France's top institutions, the city draws students from all over the world. It's this young, international crowd that keeps the city feeling fresh—new cafés open in old buildings, art exhibits pop up in forgotten courtyards, and the conversations you hear in coffee shops can range from philosophy to physics to politics.

A Gateway to the Alsace Region

As rich and vibrant as Strasbourg is, it's also the perfect base for exploring the rest of Alsace. Within an hour, you can be sipping wine in Colmar, hiking in the Vosges mountains, or touring medieval villages that look like they were lifted from the pages of a fairy tale. Trains are frequent, roads are easy to navigate, and each small town seems to have its own story to tell.

Strasbourg isn't just a destination—it's a doorway. It introduces you to a region steeped in tradition, shaped by history, and constantly looking ahead. Whether you're here for a weekend or planning a longer stay, there's always more to uncover. You could spend hours in the cathedral, days wandering through La Petite France, and still leave feeling like you've only scratched the surface.

So if you're wondering whether Strasbourg is worth your time—the answer is yes. Not because it checks every travel box, but because it writes its own list. It's historic without being stuck in the past, cultured without being pretentious, and welcoming without being over-polished. It's real, it's layered, and it's ready for you.

1.2 Why Visit Strasbourg in 2025–2026

Strasbourg isn't just worth visiting—it's *timely* to visit in 2025–2026. These two years offer a sweet spot: the post-pandemic travel scene has found its rhythm, European cities are bouncing back with vibrant cultural calendars, and Strasbourg is leading the way with a mix of tradition and innovation. Whether it's your first time or your fifth, this period brings fresh reasons to explore, eat, wander, and discover. So, why now? Let's dig into what makes Strasbourg an especially smart and satisfying choice for travel in 2025 and 2026.

1. It's the Best of France and Germany in One Place

Strasbourg doesn't sit in some cultural no-man's land—it embraces both sides of its identity. You'll find French elegance alongside German precision, Alsatian flavors blending both influences, and locals who comfortably switch between languages. For travelers, this means more variety, deeper stories, and a more complex (in a good way) cultural experience. In one afternoon, you can sip Riesling from the nearby vineyards, try a buttery kougelhopf pastry, and hear a Bach concerto performed in a Gothic church. You're not just visiting a city—you're dipping into two cultures at once.

2. Strasbourg's Old Town Is Straight Out of a Fairytale

If you've ever flipped through a book of European travel postcards, you've probably already seen bits of Strasbourg—colorful half-timbered homes lining canals, flower boxes overflowing in spring, crooked lanes with cozy cafés tucked into every corner. The *Grande Île*, the historic heart of the city, is a UNESCO World Heritage Site for a reason. It's compact, walkable, and packed with charm. But it's also lived-in and vibrant. Locals do their shopping here, students sip espresso on the cathedral steps, and on sunny days, artists sketch along the riverbanks. It's not a museum—it's a place people call home. And it's open to you.

3. The Events Calendar is Packed

In 2025 and 2026, Strasbourg's events calendar is looking especially strong. Whether you plan to visit in summer, fall, or over the holidays, there's almost always something happening:

- **Strasbourg Music Week** and open-air jazz concerts bring international and local talent into the spotlight.
- The **European Fantastic Film Festival** returns with new cinematic gems and genre surprises.

- Art exhibits rotate through the city's museums, and many public spaces transform into creative installations.
- And of course, **the famous Christmas Market**—which will be celebrating over four centuries of tradition—is an absolute highlight. Lights, mulled wine, handcrafted ornaments, choirs echoing through the squares—it's one of the most magical winter experiences you'll find anywhere in Europe.

Strasbourg doesn't just keep old traditions alive—it actively creates new ones, and visitors are always welcome to join in.

4. A European Capital with Global Relevance

Strasbourg is no ordinary small city. It plays a major role on the international stage as the official seat of the **European Parliament**, as well as home to the **Council of Europe** and **European Court of Human Rights**. That political presence brings a level of global awareness you won't always find in cities of this size. It also means you'll run into journalists, students, lawmakers, and visitors from all over the world. The city buzzes with discussion, with activism, with ideas. It's a great destination if you like cities that *think* as much as they *shine*.

Tours of the European Parliament are open to the public when in session, offering travelers a rare inside look at how decisions affecting millions of Europeans are made. In a world that's becoming more interconnected by the minute, Strasbourg offers a front-row seat to history in the making.

5. Green Travel is Easy Here

If sustainable travel is on your radar—and it probably should be—Strasbourg is a model of how to do it right. The city is famously bike-friendly, with over 600 kilometers of cycling paths, and its public transit network is one of the cleanest and most efficient in France. The tram glides quietly through the historic center, reducing car traffic and emissions. Plus, green spaces are everywhere—parks, riverside promenades, and garden walkways that make wandering around a pleasure in every season.

Travelers in 2025–2026 will find that Strasbourg continues to invest in sustainability—from hotel energy initiatives to eco-conscious dining. It's a great place to enjoy a guilt-free vacation while still seeing everything you came for.

6. New Hotels, Refreshed Museums, and Improved Access

Over the last few years, Strasbourg has quietly been upgrading its infrastructure to better serve a new wave of travelers. In 2025, several boutique hotels are opening or reopening after full renovations, offering modern comforts within charming old buildings. Museums are also seeing updates—like interactive exhibits, bilingual displays, and rotating installations that go beyond traditional formats.

There's also a stronger focus on accessibility now. Whether you're traveling with mobility challenges, kids, or specific dietary needs, you'll find more options than ever before. The local tourism board has made it easier to navigate attractions, book transportation, and find tailored experiences online—making 2025 and 2026 two of the most traveler-friendly years Strasbourg has seen.

7. Food and Wine Culture at Its Peak

Strasbourg in the coming travel years is a food lover's playground. The culinary scene is booming, with young chefs giving classic Alsatian dishes a modern twist, while traditional winstubs continue to serve hearty, comforting favorites. Expect crispy *tarte flambée*, slow-braised meats, and delicious pastries that disappear from your plate faster than you planned.

Wine lovers, take note: Alsace wines are hitting their stride with growing international recognition, and 2025–2026 will feature special events tied to local wine routes, seasonal tastings, and vineyard tours. Strasbourg acts as the starting point for the **Alsace Wine Route**, making it the perfect city to indulge and explore the region's famous whites—Riesling, Gewürztraminer, and Pinot Gris among them.

8. A Perfect Launchpad for Day Trips

Finally, one of Strasbourg's biggest strengths is its location. It's not just a destination—it's a springboard. Within an hour or two, you can be exploring medieval villages like Obernai, admiring the half-timbered houses of Colmar, soaking in spa towns, hiking through the Vosges mountains, or even hopping across the border into the Black Forest in Germany.

Strasbourg's train connections are fast and frequent, and if you prefer the scenic route, there are car rentals and bike paths that take you through rolling vineyards, castle ruins, and quiet countryside.

So, Why Visit in 2025–2026?

Because Strasbourg is ready—and it's only getting better. The crowds are manageable, the infrastructure is polished, and the energy in the city is as bright as ever. Whether you're here to explore history, sip wine, attend a festival, or just relax along a quiet canal with a book, Strasbourg will deliver—and then some.

In the end, it's not just about seeing a place. It's about *feeling* it. And Strasbourg? It stays with you.

1.3 Key Facts and Quick Tips

This section provides essential facts and practical advice to assist travelers in planning and navigating their visit to Strasbourg. Whether preparing for a short stay or an extended visit, the information below serves as a comprehensive reference point for logistical, cultural, and situational awareness.

General Information

- **Country**: France
- **Region**: Grand Est (formerly Alsace)
- **Administrative Division**: Bas-Rhin Department
- **City Population**: Approx. 290,000 (Metropolitan Area: ~800,000)
- **Official Language**: French
- **Common Regional Languages**: Alsatian (a Germanic dialect), German (limited)

- **Currency**: Euro (€)
- **Time Zone**: Central European Time (CET, UTC+1) / Central European Summer Time (CEST, UTC+2)
- **International Dialing Code**: +33 (France), local area code (0)3
- **Official Website**: strasbourg.eu

Optimal Time to Visit

Strasbourg can be enjoyed year-round, but specific seasons offer distinct advantages:

- **Spring (March–May)**: Mild temperatures and blooming landscapes make this an excellent time for sightseeing, outdoor cafés, and early festivals. Crowds are moderate.
- **Summer (June–August)**: Ideal for open-air events, walking tours, and river cruises. Expect higher tourist volume, particularly in July and August.
- **Autumn (September–November)**: Grape harvest season in the surrounding Alsace region, with colorful foliage and wine festivals. A quieter period with mild weather.
- **Winter (December–February)**: Strasbourg's renowned Christmas markets transform the city into a festive setting. Cold temperatures are offset by holiday ambiance, especially in December.

Getting There

By Air

- **Strasbourg Airport (SXB)**: Located approximately 15 minutes from the city center by shuttle or train. Serves regional and limited international routes.
- **Nearby Major Airports**:
  - EuroAirport Basel–Mulhouse–Freiburg (approx. 90 minutes by train)
  - Frankfurt International Airport (approx. 2 hours by train)

By Train

- **High-Speed Rail (TGV)** provides efficient service:
  - Paris to Strasbourg: ~1 hour 45 minutes
  - Frankfurt to Strasbourg: ~2 hours
  - Luxembourg to Strasbourg: ~2 hours 15 minutes

By Road

- Accessible via A4 and A35 highways from major cities in France and Germany. Driving through the Alsace region offers scenic vineyard routes.

By Bus

- Long-distance coach services such as FlixBus and BlaBlaCar Bus offer budget-friendly travel but take longer than trains.

Local Transportation

Public Transit

- Strasbourg's public transport is managed by the CTS (Compagnie des Transports Strasbourgeois), covering both trams and buses.
  - A single-ride ticket costs €1.90; day and multi-day passes are available.
  - Tickets must be validated upon entry.

Cycling

- Strasbourg is one of the most bike-friendly cities in France.
  - **Vélhop** is the primary bike rental system, with short- and long-term rental options.
  - Over 600 kilometers of bike paths are maintained throughout the city and suburbs.

Walking

- The city center, especially Grande Île, is highly walkable. Many key attractions are within short walking distances.

Taxi and Ride-Sharing

- Taxis are readily available but relatively costly.
- Uber operates in Strasbourg with moderate availability, especially near central districts.

Cultural Etiquette and Practical Norms

- **Language**: While French is the official language, English is widely spoken in hotels, restaurants, and tourism-related services. Learning a few basic French greetings is appreciated by locals.

- **Dining Customs**: Meals are a leisurely affair. Waitstaff typically wait for guests to request the bill (*l'addition, s'il vous plaît*). Tipping is not required but is customary to round up or leave small change.
- **Business Hours**:
  - Most shops close on Sundays, except during seasonal events.
  - Lunchtime closures (12:00 p.m. – 2:00 p.m.) are common in small boutiques.
  - Malls and supermarkets generally stay open later, including some Sundays.
- **Noise Ordinance**: Quiet hours are enforced from 10:00 p.m. to 7:00 a.m., especially in residential areas.

Safety and Health

- Strasbourg is generally safe, with a low violent crime rate.
  - Be mindful of petty theft in crowded areas or during events (e.g., Christmas market).
- **Emergency Numbers**:
  - Police: 17
  - Ambulance: 15
  - Fire: 18
  - European emergency number (EU-wide): 112
- **Pharmacies**: Identified by a green cross. Most pharmacists speak basic English and provide over-the-counter medical advice.
- **Water Quality**: Tap water is safe for drinking throughout the city.

Budget Overview (Per Person, Per Day)

- **Economy** (€50–€80): Hostel or budget hotel, fast-casual meals, museum access, public transport pass.
- **Mid-range** (€100–€180): Three-star accommodation, sit-down meals, wine tasting, river cruise.
- **Luxury** (€200+): Four-star or boutique hotel, fine dining, guided tours, shopping.

Technology and Mobile Tools

Recommended apps for visitors:

- **CTS Strasbourg**: Public transport schedules, ticket purchases

- **Vélhop**: Bike rentals and location maps
- **TheFork**: Restaurant reservations and user reviews
- **Google Maps / Maps.me**: City navigation
- **Google Translate**: Language translation for menus and signs

Strasbourg Pass

The **Strasbourg Pass** is an official tourism product offering excellent value for short-term visitors. Benefits include:

- Free admission to select museums
- One riverboat cruise
- Reduced fares for guided tours and cathedral access
- Valid for 1, 2, or 3 days
  Available at the Strasbourg Tourist Office and online.

Local Terms and Menu Vocabulary

Familiarity with a few Alsatian or French terms enhances the travel experience:

- **Winstub** – Traditional Alsatian tavern
- **Tarte flambée / Flammekueche** – Alsatian-style flatbread
- **Baeckeoffe** – Alsatian meat and vegetable stew
- **Kougelhopf** – Sweet or savory yeasted cake
- **Place** – Town square (e.g., Place Kléber)
- **Rue** – Street
- **Cathédrale** – Cathedral

Insider Tips

- **Book Early**: Popular accommodations and restaurants fill up quickly during peak seasons, especially in December and summer months.
- **Strasbourg–Kehl Tram Connection**: Take Tram Line D to visit Kehl, Germany—just across the Rhine. No border check required.
- **Layered Clothing**: Weather can shift throughout the day, especially in spring and fall.
- **Avoid Rush Hour**: Trams and buses are most congested from 7:30–9:00 a.m. and 5:00–6:30 p.m.
- **Cultural Events**: Look out for seasonal events such as the Christmas Market, European Night of Museums, and summer concerts in Place du Château.

Chapter 2: Planning Your Trip

2.1 Best Time to Visit Strasbourg

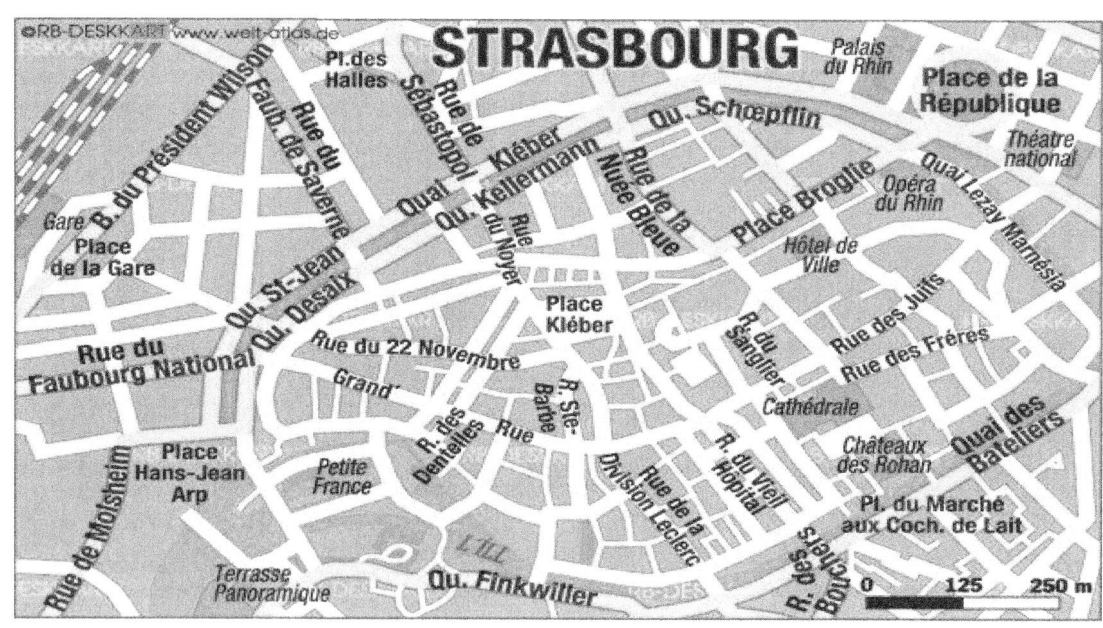

Strasbourg is one of those rare cities that can be rewarding to visit at virtually any time of the year. Thanks to its unique blend of French and German influences, well-preserved architecture, and a calendar rich with seasonal events, the city offers something distinct in every season. Choosing the best time to go largely depends on what kind of traveler you are and what sort of experience you're after. Do you prefer vibrant festivals and sunny days? Are you drawn to quiet alleyways dusted with snow and the magic of Christmas lights? Or do you simply want to avoid crowds while still enjoying comfortable weather and cultural depth? Let's walk through the seasons so you can decide when Strasbourg is at its best—for you.

Spring (March to May)

Spring is a wonderfully refreshing time to visit Strasbourg. As the frost retreats and the city emerges from its winter slumber, public gardens begin to bloom, outdoor cafés come back to life, and the air carries a sense of renewal. March can still be quite brisk and somewhat gray, especially in the early days, but by April the city is bursting with greenery and blossoms. The banks of the Ill River become especially scenic, and parks like Parc de l'Orangerie are dotted with blooming magnolias and tulips.

This is a great time for those who enjoy walking tours and sightseeing without the heavy summer foot traffic. Prices for flights and hotels tend to be more favorable during this shoulder season, particularly in March and April. Late April and early May often bring a few regional festivals and food markets, including early wine celebrations that reflect Alsace's deep viticultural roots. The Easter season can get a bit busy due to local celebrations and school holidays, but overall, spring remains one of the most balanced and enjoyable times to explore the city.

Summer (June to August)

If you love sunshine, long days, and a lively urban atmosphere, summer is likely your best bet. Strasbourg during the summer is energetic and packed with activity. Streets are filled with locals and tourists, boats glide up and down the canals, and sidewalk terraces hum with conversation well into the night. With average highs ranging between the mid-70s and low 80s Fahrenheit (24–28°C), the weather is generally ideal for walking, biking, and open-air markets.

The summer months also bring a full lineup of events. Outdoor concerts, arts festivals, and cultural performances pop up throughout the city. National Day on July 14 is celebrated in grand fashion, with fireworks and public gatherings adding to the festive mood. Museums and tourist attractions are fully operational and often extend their hours to accommodate the crowds.

That said, summer is also Strasbourg's peak tourist season. Expect higher accommodation prices, longer lines at major landmarks like Strasbourg Cathedral, and busy days in the city center—especially in La Petite France. If you want the summer atmosphere but without quite as many people, early June is an excellent window to target. August can be hit or miss, as some local businesses may close for their own holidays, though major attractions stay open.

Autumn (September to November)

Autumn in Strasbourg is arguably one of the most charming times to visit, especially for those who appreciate cultural depth and a slower pace. The weather stays mild through much of September, and by October, the city and surrounding countryside take on rich shades of gold, amber, and rust. The wine harvest season adds a unique flavor to the region, quite literally—nearby vineyards host tastings, and local restaurants highlight seasonal ingredients like mushrooms, game, and squash.

September offers an excellent mix of favorable weather, fewer tourists, and vibrant color. The city feels more lived-in, as students return and locals settle into the rhythms of the season. This is also a prime time for photography, as the light softens and the historic buildings are framed by fall foliage.

By November, things quieted down significantly. The days grow shorter, temperatures dip, and the tourist flow slows to a trickle. But this is also the month when Strasbourg begins its transformation into a winter wonderland, with lights and decorations going up ahead of the famous Christmas market. If you're someone who enjoys a quieter, more atmospheric cityscape, late autumn can be deeply rewarding.

Winter (December to February)

There's no question that December is a magical time in Strasbourg. The city is world-renowned for its Christmas market, known locally as the *Christkindelsmärik*, which dates back to 1570 and is considered one of the oldest in Europe. During the holiday season, the entire historic center is transformed into a fairy-tale setting, complete with glowing lights, decorated fir trees, carolers, and more than 300 wooden chalets offering everything from handmade ornaments to warm mulled wine and traditional Alsatian pastries.

The holiday atmosphere is unlike anything else in France, and it draws visitors from across the globe. Accommodations tend to book out months in advance, and prices are at their highest, especially during weekends in December. Still, if you want that festive feeling, it's well worth the planning and investment.

Once the holiday season ends, typically just after New Year's Day, Strasbourg slows down again. January and February are much quieter, and while the cold can be biting, especially at night, this is when you can see the city's cultural side without the distractions of large crowds. Museum exhibitions, classical concerts, and theater performances continue through winter, and hotels often offer better rates. It's also a peaceful time to enjoy cozy Alsatian restaurants, many of which are at their most inviting during the colder months.

Final Thoughts on Timing Your Trip

There's no universally perfect time to visit Strasbourg, but there is an ideal time depending on your goals. If you're after lively festivals, bustling markets, and warm outdoor evenings, then summer is your season. If you're more interested in wine, seasonal foods, and a quieter urban experience, then autumn is a top choice. Winter is best for those who want to soak in the festive charm of the Christmas markets or enjoy the city without crowds in the post-holiday lull. Spring, meanwhile, offers a bit of everything—beauty, balance, and manageable tourism levels.

It's also worth considering your tolerance for weather conditions. Strasbourg, being located near the Rhine River and close to the Vosges Mountains, can be humid in summer and brisk in winter. Rain is possible in every season, so bringing a lightweight raincoat or umbrella is always a smart idea, no matter when you travel.

Ultimately, the best time to visit Strasbourg is when the city's seasonal offerings align with what you're hoping to get out of your trip—whether that's sipping Riesling in a quiet autumn café, strolling through medieval lanes draped in spring blossoms, or marveling at cathedral spires dusted with snow and holiday lights.

2.2 Visa Requirements & Entry Rules

When planning a trip to Strasbourg in 2025 or 2026, understanding the visa requirements and entry regulations is crucial for a smooth and stress-free journey. Since Strasbourg is located in northeastern France—just a few miles from the German border—it falls under the jurisdiction of France's immigration policies, which are governed by the broader rules of the **Schengen Area**. These rules apply uniformly across 27 European countries that have abolished passport control at their mutual borders.

Your visa obligations will depend on your nationality, the length and purpose of your stay, and whether you've visited Schengen countries recently. This section outlines all key entry protocols travelers should be aware of, from short-stay tourist visas to special rules for digital nomads, students, or frequent visitors.

Understanding the Schengen Area and Strasbourg's Status

Strasbourg is in France and therefore part of the **Schengen Agreement**, a treaty that allows border-free travel between participating countries. This means if you're entering Strasbourg from another Schengen country, such as Germany, Switzerland, or Belgium, you won't be required to go through passport control again.

If you're arriving directly into France from a non-Schengen country, such as the United Kingdom, the United States, Canada, India, Australia, or China, then French border control will handle your immigration process. This is where your passport, visa (if required), and supporting documents will be checked.

Visa-Free Entry for Short Stays (Up to 90 Days)

Nationals from many countries **do not need a visa** to enter Strasbourg (and the rest of France) for stays up to **90 days within a 180-day period**. These include:

- United States
- Canada
- United Kingdom (post-Brexit)
- Australia
- New Zealand
- Japan
- South Korea
- Singapore
- Most countries in Latin America

If you are from one of these visa-exempt countries, you can visit Strasbourg for tourism, business meetings, short-term education, or family visits without applying for a visa. You'll only need:

- A passport valid for at least three months beyond your departure date from the Schengen Area
- Proof of onward or return travel
- Proof of accommodation (hotel reservations, invitation letter, etc.)
- Sufficient financial means for the duration of your stay
- Travel insurance (strongly recommended, and may become required with ETIAS)

You cannot legally work or study long-term on a visa-free entry.

ETIAS Travel Authorization (Starting 2025)

By the time you travel in **2025 or 2026**, travelers from visa-exempt countries will be subject to a new requirement: the **ETIAS system** (*European Travel Information and Authorization System*). This is **not a visa**, but a mandatory online pre-travel authorization meant to strengthen security within the Schengen Zone.

If you're from a visa-exempt country, you must apply online for ETIAS before traveling. Here's what you need to know:

- Application is done online via the official ETIAS portal
- Fee: Approx. €7 per adult (free for minors and seniors over 70)
- Valid for multiple entries over three years or until your passport expires
- You must apply at least **a few days before departure** (though most applications are approved within minutes)
- You'll receive digital confirmation—no physical documents required

ETIAS goes into full effect in 2025, so it will apply to nearly all non-EU tourists visiting Strasbourg starting that year.

Visa Requirements for Non-Visa-Exempt Travelers

If you're from a country that does not have a visa exemption agreement with the Schengen Zone (e.g., India, Nigeria, Pakistan, South Africa, and many others), you will need to apply for a Schengen visa in advance from the French consulate or embassy in your country.

Requirements typically include:

- A valid passport (with at least two blank pages and validity 3 months past your planned exit date)
- Completed **Schengen visa application form**
- Recent passport-sized photos
- Proof of accommodation and travel itinerary
- Round-trip flight reservations
- Travel medical insurance with minimum coverage of €30,000
- Financial proof of funds (bank statements, sponsorship letter)
- Application fee: approx. €80 (varies slightly by country and circumstances)

Processing time can take from 10–30 days, so apply well in advance of your planned trip.

A short-stay Schengen visa allows you to stay up to 90 days within any 180-day period across the entire Schengen Zone. If you want to stay longer—for study, work, or family reunification—you'll need a long-stay national visa, issued specifically by the French authorities.

Entry for Long-Term Stays

If your visit to Strasbourg will exceed 90 days, or if your reason for visiting involves employment, education, research, or residency, you must apply for a long-stay visa or residency permit. France offers several visa categories based on purpose:

- **Student Visa** – For full-time academic programs
- **Work Visa** – Must be sponsored by an employer in France
- **Talent Passport** – For entrepreneurs, artists, and researchers
- **Au Pair Visa** – For cultural exchange and part-time work with a host family
- **Family Reunification** – If you're joining close relatives residing in France

Each visa category has specific requirements and documentation, and some may involve additional administrative steps once you arrive (such as registering with local immigration offices or undergoing a medical check).

Border Checks and Entry Process

Upon arrival in France (if you're coming from outside the Schengen Zone), border officers may ask for:

- Your passport (with appropriate visa, if required)
- Proof of accommodation and return travel
- Financial support documentation
- Proof of travel health insurance
- ETIAS approval, if applicable

It's recommended to carry paper or digital copies of all these documents, even if you're not usually asked to present them. French immigration officials have the discretion to deny entry if your documentation is incomplete or your intentions are unclear.

Traveling Within Schengen After Entering France

Once you enter Strasbourg legally through a Schengen port of entry, you're free to travel throughout the other 26 Schengen countries without additional border checks. This makes Strasbourg an excellent starting point for a wider European adventure, particularly to nearby destinations like:

- **Germany** – Just across the Rhine River
- **Switzerland** – A few hours south by train
- **Belgium and Luxembourg** – Easily reachable by rail or car

Do keep track of your total time spent in the Schengen Zone to avoid overstaying the permitted 90 days in any rolling 180-day period.

Special Notes for UK Citizens (Post-Brexit)

Since Brexit, UK nationals are **no longer EU citizens** and are treated like other visa-exempt nationals. This means:

- UK citizens can stay up to 90 days in any 180-day period
- ETIAS authorization will be required starting in 2025
- Working, studying, or staying longer than 90 days requires a visa

While British travelers enjoy relatively smooth access to France, you must still comply with all new regulations introduced since Brexit.

Final Entry Tips

- Always check the official French consulate or embassy website in your country for the most current rules before applying for a visa.
- Remember that rules can change with new EU policies, so staying updated—especially as the ETIAS system comes into full force—is essential.
- If you plan to cross borders frequently or stay in Europe for an extended period, **keep track of your days** to avoid overstaying.

Planning ahead and understanding your entry requirements will save you time, stress, and potentially costly issues at the border. With the right documents in hand, you'll be well on your way to enjoying everything Strasbourg has to offer.

2.3 Budgeting & Currency

Creating a realistic budget is one of the most important aspects of planning your trip to Strasbourg. While France as a whole is often perceived as an expensive destination, Strasbourg offers a wide range of options for travelers of all budgets. From charming boutique hotels and Michelin-starred restaurants to casual bistros and budget-friendly accommodations, the city caters to a wide audience. The key is knowing how to allocate your spending and what to expect in terms of pricing across different categories—accommodation, food, transportation, sightseeing, and miscellaneous costs.

This section offers a comprehensive breakdown of Strasbourg's cost landscape, as well as practical currency advice to help you manage your finances wisely during your 2025–2026 visit.

The Currency: Euro (€)

Strasbourg, like the rest of France, uses the **euro (EUR)** as its official currency. It's a widely accepted and stable currency used across 20 of the 27 European Union countries, making it convenient for travelers planning multi-country itineraries. Euro banknotes come in denominations of €5, €10, €20, €50, €100, €200, and €500, though the larger denominations are not commonly used for everyday transactions. Coins range from 1 cent to €2.

When budgeting, it's helpful to remember that Strasbourg is located near the German border, where the euro is also used, so currency exchange won't be necessary if you're crossing into or coming from Germany.

Average Daily Budget Ranges (2025–2026)

Your daily expenses in Strasbourg can vary significantly based on your travel style. Here's a breakdown of typical daily budgets:

- **Budget Travelers (€50–€80/day)**
  - Hostels or budget hotels
  - Public transportation or walking
  - Self-catering or takeout meals
  - Free or low-cost attractions (museums with free entry days, parks, markets)
- **Mid-Range Travelers (€100–€180/day)**
  - Comfortable 3-star hotels or vacation rentals
  - Mix of public transit and occasional taxis
  - Sit-down meals at local bistros
  - Admission to museums, boat rides, guided walking tours
- **Luxury Travelers (€250–€500+/day)**
  - Boutique hotels or 4–5 star accommodations
  - Private transfers or rental cars
  - Fine dining and wine pairings
  - Private tours, cultural shows, and shopping at high-end boutiques

Traveling during peak holiday seasons (e.g., summer, Christmas markets) will raise accommodation and airfare prices significantly, so plan accordingly.

Accommodation Costs

Accommodation in Strasbourg ranges from budget hostels and affordable apartments to luxurious riverside hotels and historic inns in the heart of the old town. On average:

- **Budget hostels and 2-star hotels:** €40–€70 per night
- **Mid-range 3-star hotels or well-rated Airbnbs:** €90–€140 per night
- **Luxury hotels or boutique stays:** €180–€400+ per night

If you're traveling on a budget, book well in advance, especially during the Christmas season or during the Strasbourg European Parliament sessions, when hotels fill up quickly.

Meals & Dining Costs

Strasbourg's cuisine is a highlight of any visit, combining French elegance with German heartiness. You can eat well here on any budget.

- **Bakeries and quick meals:** €4–€10 for a sandwich, pastry, or kebab
- **Casual cafés or bistros:** €12–€20 for a set lunch menu
- **Brasseries and winstubs (Alsatian taverns):** €25–€40 per person for a full meal with drinks
- **Fine dining or Michelin-starred restaurants:** €80–€200+ per person

A great way to save is by choosing the **formula du midi** (lunch specials) which many restaurants offer—often a two- or three-course meal for a fraction of the dinner price.

Transportation Expenses

Getting around Strasbourg is straightforward and relatively affordable. The city is compact and pedestrian-friendly, but it also boasts an efficient tram and bus system.

- **Single tram/bus ticket:** €1.80 (€1.70 if bought in bulk)
- **24-hour pass:** Around €4.60 (unlimited use)
- **Bike rental:** €10–€15 per day via Vélhop public bike-sharing system
- **Taxi base fare:** Around €7, plus €1.50–€2/km

If you plan to explore beyond Strasbourg—such as day trips to Colmar or the Alsace Wine Route—set aside money for **regional train fares**, which can range from €10 to €25 round-trip depending on distance and time of booking.

Attractions & Sightseeing

Strasbourg offers a mix of free, moderately priced, and premium attractions:

- **Free activities:** Strolling through Petite France, the Strasbourg Cathedral (entry is free), historic squares, and riverside walks
- **Museum admissions:** Typically range from €6 to €12
- **Boat tours on the Ill River:** Around €14–€16
- **Guided city tours or wine tastings:** €25–€60 depending on the experience
- **European Parliament visits:** Free, though advance booking is often required

If you plan to visit multiple museums and sites, consider the Strasbourg City Pass—valid for three days and includes discounts or free entry to many major attractions and public transit.

Tipping Culture

In France, service charges are typically included in the bill, especially in restaurants. Still, it's customary (though not obligatory) to round up the bill or leave a small tip for good service.

- **Restaurants:** Round up or leave 5–10%
- **Cafés:** €1–€2 if table service
- **Taxis:** Round up to the nearest euro or add 5–10%
- **Hotel staff:** €1–€2 per bag for porters; €5–€10 for housekeeping at checkout

Tipping is always appreciated but not expected the way it might be in the U.S.

Currency Exchange & Using Cards

ATMs are widely available across Strasbourg, especially in the city center, train stations, and shopping districts. Withdrawals usually offer better exchange rates than airport currency kiosks, though your home bank may charge international fees.

- **Credit & debit cards** (Visa and Mastercard in particular) are widely accepted at hotels, restaurants, and shops.
- **Contactless payments** are commonly used for public transit, cafés, and small purchases.
- American Express may be less commonly accepted, particularly at smaller establishments.

Always notify your bank in advance if you're traveling internationally to avoid transaction blocks. It's also wise to carry a small amount of cash for street markets, small cafés, or tips.

Money-Saving Tips

- **Book accommodation early**, especially for travel during the Christmas market season or summer holidays.
- **Travel in the shoulder season** (April–May or September–October) for lower prices and fewer crowds.
- **Take advantage of combo passes** like the Strasbourg City Pass for attractions.

- **Eat like a local:** Head to bakeries for breakfast, grab lunch specials, and explore winstubs instead of tourist-trap restaurants.
- **Use public transportation or rent a bike** instead of relying on taxis.

Final Thoughts on Budgeting

Strasbourg doesn't require a lavish budget to enjoy its culture, cuisine, and charm. With careful planning, even a modest budget can go a long way, especially if you're flexible with your travel dates and dining choices. Whether you're a backpacker on a tight schedule or a traveler seeking refined comfort, understanding the local costs and currency norms will help ensure your trip is both enjoyable and financially manageable.

2.4 Travel Insurance & Health Tips

When planning your trip to Strasbourg, travel insurance and personal health preparedness should never be an afterthought. While France is known for its high standards in healthcare and safety, unforeseen circumstances such as illness, injury, trip cancellations, or lost luggage can occur anywhere. Travel insurance serves as a safeguard—not just for financial protection but also for peace of mind.

This section walks you through the essentials of travel insurance and health-related preparations specific to Strasbourg and France at large, ensuring you're well-informed before and during your stay.

Why Travel Insurance Is Essential

No one expects things to go wrong while traveling, but disruptions are always a possibility. Whether it's a missed connecting flight, a twisted ankle while strolling through Petite France, or a sudden illness that requires urgent care, the costs—especially for non-residents—can add up quickly without proper coverage.

A comprehensive travel insurance policy is especially valuable for:

- Medical emergencies and hospitalization
- Trip cancellations or interruptions
- Lost or delayed baggage
- Flight delays and missed connections
- Theft or loss of personal belongings
- Personal liability coverage
- COVID-19-related issues (if still applicable)

Most French healthcare facilities require upfront payment if you are uninsured, and fees—even in public hospitals—can be significant for foreigners. Having coverage will not only ensure you're reimbursed but can also connect you with multilingual assistance and local doctors.

What to Look for in a Travel Insurance Policy

When shopping for a policy, be sure it includes:

- **Emergency medical coverage**: At least €100,000 in medical coverage is recommended. Ensure this includes outpatient treatment, emergency surgeries, hospital stays, and medical evacuation.
- **Trip cancellation and interruption**: Protects your investment if unexpected events force you to change your plans before or during travel.
- **24/7 assistance services**: Many insurers offer emergency hotlines to help coordinate local care, locate nearby hospitals, or replace lost documents.
- **Repatriation**: In the unlikely event of severe illness or death, this coverage ensures safe transportation back to your home country.
- **COVID-19 coverage**: Although restrictions have eased, some providers continue to include COVID-19 testing, quarantine costs, or cancellation protection if you contract the virus before or during travel.

Optional add-ons may include protection for high-risk activities (like skiing in the Vosges Mountains), adventure sports, rental cars, and electronic gear.

Always read the fine print carefully, noting any exclusions or limitations based on pre-existing conditions, age, trip length, or destination risk level.

Vaccination Requirements & General Health Advice

There are no mandatory vaccines required for travelers entering France from most countries, but keeping your routine vaccinations up to date is highly recommended. These include:

- **MMR (Measles, Mumps, Rubella)**
- **Tetanus-Diphtheria-Pertussis**
- **Polio**
- **Influenza (seasonal flu)** — especially for winter travelers
- **COVID-19** — depending on global and EU travel regulations at the time

Travelers with chronic health conditions should carry a letter from their physician detailing their medical history, prescribed medications (with generic names), and emergency instructions if applicable.

If you take prescription medication, bring enough for the entire trip—plus a little extra in case of delays—along with a copy of the prescription. All medication should be transported in original packaging and carried in hand luggage.

Healthcare in Strasbourg

France is known for having one of the best healthcare systems in the world, and Strasbourg is no exception. The city is home to well-equipped hospitals, private clinics, and 24-hour pharmacies. Many healthcare professionals, especially in urban centers like Strasbourg, speak at least some English, although not all staff may be fluent.

Key medical institutions in Strasbourg include:

- **Nouvel Hôpital Civil (NHC)** – One of the largest public hospitals in eastern France
- **Clinique Rhéna** – A reputable private clinic offering specialized services
- **Centre Médical Europe** – Known for treating international visitors and multilingual assistance

For minor ailments, local pharmacies are a good first stop. French pharmacists are highly trained and can offer reliable medical advice or suggest over-the-counter treatments. Many pharmacies display a green illuminated cross outside, and emergency pharmacies operate nights and weekends on a rotating basis.

Emergency Numbers & Services

It's helpful to know the main emergency contact numbers in France:

- **112** – Universal emergency number (can be dialed from any EU country)
- **15** – Medical emergency (SAMU)
- **17** – Police
- **18** – Fire brigade
- **116 117** – Non-urgent medical assistance (especially outside regular clinic hours)

Many hotels, tourist offices, and transportation hubs will have emergency contact information posted or available upon request. It's also wise to keep a printed copy of your insurance details and emergency contacts with you at all times.

Staying Healthy During Your Trip

Strasbourg is a safe and clean city, but like anywhere, taking basic precautions can help you avoid unnecessary health issues.

- **Drink bottled water** if you prefer, though tap water in Strasbourg is completely safe and meets EU quality standards.
- **Pack a mini first-aid kit**: Include pain relievers, anti-diarrheal medicine, hand sanitizer, blister plasters, and motion sickness pills if you plan on taking day trips through winding countryside roads.
- **Practice food safety**: Alsatian cuisine is hearty and rich. If you have a sensitive stomach, ease into the regional diet to avoid digestive upset.
- **Watch for seasonal illnesses**: In colder months, flu and colds are more common. Wear layers, practice good hygiene, and consider a flu shot if traveling during winter.
- **Use insect repellent in warmer months**, especially if you're venturing outside the city into rural or vineyard areas.

Tips for Travelers with Special Health Needs

- **Wheelchair accessibility**: Strasbourg has made significant strides in improving accessibility, particularly in public transportation and key cultural sites. Tram stations are generally wheelchair-accessible, and many attractions offer accommodations.

- **Dietary restrictions**: Supermarkets and restaurants in Strasbourg increasingly cater to gluten-free, vegetarian, vegan, and allergy-friendly diets. Always confirm with staff and use translation apps if needed.
- **Mental health support**: If you're traveling long-term or have mental health needs, several English-speaking therapists are available in Strasbourg, and many insurance policies cover remote consultations.

Final Notes on Health & Safety

While Strasbourg is not a risky destination, unexpected health-related events can turn a trip upside down if you're not adequately prepared. A small investment in a comprehensive travel insurance plan and a proactive approach to your personal health can protect both your finances and your well-being. From reliable emergency services to top-notch hospitals and pharmacies, Strasbourg has the infrastructure to care for visitors—provided you're ready with the right tools and information.

Before departure, make a checklist: insurance confirmation, a list of medications, contact numbers, and copies of important documents. That way, even in the event of a setback, you can travel with confidence and peace of mind.

Chapter 3: Getting to Strasbourg

3.1 By Air: Strasbourg Airport & Nearby Hubs

Arriving in Strasbourg by air can be seamless and efficient, whether you're flying from within Europe or connecting from another continent. While Strasbourg itself has a modest but well-equipped airport, many international travelers opt to fly into larger neighboring hubs and connect to Strasbourg via France's robust rail network or the European highway system. This section explores both direct and indirect air routes in detail, highlighting what you can expect at each airport, how to transition smoothly between air and ground transport, and how to choose the best airport based on your travel profile.

Strasbourg Entzheim Airport (SXB)

Located just under 10 kilometers southwest of the city center, **Strasbourg Entzheim Airport (Aéroport de Strasbourg)** is the closest airport to the city and offers a convenient entry point for those traveling from other European destinations. It is a mid-sized regional airport, efficient and user-friendly, primarily handling short-haul and domestic flights.

Airlines & Routes

SXB is not a major international hub, but it does serve key European cities. You'll find regular flights to and from:

- **Paris (CDG and Orly)**
- **Amsterdam**
- **Madrid**
- **Marseille**
- **Nice**
- **Toulouse**
- **Lyon**
- **Lisbon**

Airlines frequently operating out of SXB include:

- **Air France** (domestic and European routes)
- **Volotea** (seasonal Mediterranean destinations)
- **Ryanair** (low-cost options)
- **Lufthansa** (feeder flights to Frankfurt or Munich)

Terminal Services & Facilities

Despite its smaller scale, Strasbourg Airport offers all the basic amenities:

- **Free Wi-Fi throughout the terminal**
- **Rental car agencies** on-site (Avis, Hertz, Europcar, Sixt)
- **Cafés and snack bars** for travelers waiting on flights
- **Currency exchange kiosks and ATMs**
- **Duty-free shopping** for international flights
- **Passenger assistance services** for those with mobility needs

The airport has a reputation for being clean, efficient, and easy to navigate. Lines for check-in and security are usually short, which makes it an attractive option for quick arrivals and departures.

Ground Transportation Options

Once you land at SXB, you have multiple options to reach the city center:

- **Train**: Perhaps the most efficient method. The airport connects to the Strasbourg central train station via a short shuttle to Entzheim Station. Trains depart every 15–20 minutes during the day, and the ride takes about 9 minutes.
- **Taxi**: Taxis are readily available outside the terminal. Expect to pay around €30–€40 to reach central Strasbourg, depending on the time of day.
- **Uber & Ride-Hailing Apps**: Uber is available in Strasbourg and functions reliably from the airport.
- **Car Rentals**: Ideal for travelers planning road trips through Alsace. The drive to Strasbourg city center typically takes less than 20 minutes on the A35 motorway.

Major Nearby Airports with International Connections

While SXB is perfect for European arrivals, travelers from outside Europe or those seeking more flight choices often land at one of several major international airports within a 2–4 hour radius of Strasbourg. Thanks to France's TGV high-speed rail system and its position near the German border, these options are easily accessible.

Paris Charles de Gaulle Airport (CDG) – France

Distance from Strasbourg: ~490 km
Travel Time to Strasbourg by TGV: Around 2 hours (direct)

Charles de Gaulle Airport is France's largest international airport and among the busiest in Europe. It serves as the primary arrival point for most transatlantic flights and long-haul intercontinental routes.

Key Benefits:

- Extensive global connections
- Direct high-speed train to Strasbourg from CDG's in-terminal **Gare Aéroport Charles de Gaulle 2 TGV**
- Several trains daily, making it easy to catch a connection even after a long-haul flight

Tip: If you're arriving from the U.S., Canada, Asia, or the Middle East, this is often your most straightforward option. Booking a combined air-and-rail itinerary through Air France or SNCF is highly recommended for a smooth transfer.

Frankfurt am Main Airport (FRA) – Germany

Distance from Strasbourg: ~220 km
Travel Time to Strasbourg: 2.5–3.5 hours (via train or car)

Frankfurt is Germany's largest airport and one of Europe's central aviation hubs. It offers a massive range of direct flights across the globe and is especially convenient for North American and Asian travelers.

3.2 By Train: National & International Routes

Strasbourg's location at the crossroads of Western and Central Europe makes it a significant railway hub, with robust connections across France and neighboring countries. As the capital of the Grand Est region and the seat of major European institutions, Strasbourg is exceptionally well integrated into the European high-speed and regional rail network. For both domestic and international travelers, arriving by train offers an efficient, comfortable, and environmentally friendly alternative to air or road travel.

This section provides a detailed overview of accessing Strasbourg by rail—highlighting major routes, high-speed services, international connections, station amenities, ticketing guidance, and practical tips for train travelers.

Strasbourg-Ville Railway Station: The Central Gateway

Strasbourg's principal train station, **Gare de Strasbourg-Ville**, is a vital transportation hub located within walking distance of the historic city center. The station blends modern infrastructure with preserved 19th-century architecture, housed under an impressive glass canopy. It handles more than 20 million passengers annually and supports high-speed, regional, and international routes.

Key features of Strasbourg-Ville Station include:

- Direct tram, bus, and taxi access from the station forecourt
- On-site facilities: ticket counters, multilingual signage, restrooms, cafés, convenience stores, and ATMs
- Left-luggage lockers for short- and medium-term storage
- Wi-Fi availability and digital departure boards
- Accessibility services for travelers with reduced mobility

Its central location makes the station an ideal starting point for exploring the city and the surrounding Alsace region.

Domestic Rail Travel: High-Speed TGV Services

Strasbourg is a major stop on the **TGV (Train à Grande Vitesse)** network, linking it to key French cities in under a few hours. These high-speed trains offer frequent, punctual service with modern amenities, making train travel across France exceptionally convenient.

Key TGV Connections to Strasbourg:

- **Paris (Gare de l'Est):** Approximately 1 hour 45 minutes; frequent direct service daily
- **Lyon:** Around 3 hours 45 minutes; several departures daily via Dijon or Mulhouse
- **Marseille:** Just over 6 hours; direct and connecting options
- **Lille:** Between 3 hours 30 minutes and 4 hours 10 minutes
- **Bordeaux / Nantes / Rennes:** Between 5.5 and 6.5 hours, often with a transfer in Paris

Travelers are advised to book TGV tickets in advance, especially during peak travel periods, as prices tend to increase closer to the departure date. Bookings can be made through **SNCF Connect**, **Trainline**, or affiliated railway sites.

International Rail Links: Germany, Switzerland, Luxembourg, and Belgium

Strasbourg's strategic location on the Franco-German border allows seamless train travel across Western Europe. The city is directly served by high-speed and regional trains from major international destinations.

Germany – ICE and Cross-Border TGV Services

Strasbourg is connected to several German cities via **ICE (InterCity Express)** and TGV trains through coordinated services between Deutsche Bahn (DB) and SNCF.

Key connections include:

- **Frankfurt (Main):** Approx. 2 to 2.5 hours
- **Stuttgart:** Approx. 1 hour 20 minutes to 1 hour 40 minutes
- **Munich:** Typically 3.5 to 5 hours with a transfer in Stuttgart
- **Karlsruhe:** Approx. 1 hour via regional trains or direct services

These trains are known for speed, comfort, and reliability. Cross-border agreements allow for integrated ticketing, making international journeys seamless.

Switzerland – SBB and TGV Lyria

Trains from Switzerland offer reliable access to Strasbourg via Basel or Mulhouse:

- **Basel SBB:** Around 1 hour 20 minutes
- **Zurich:** Approximately 2.5 to 3.5 hours with a change in Basel

These services are particularly useful for travelers touring multiple countries or accessing the Swiss Alps.

Luxembourg

Regional trains operated by **CFL (Luxembourg Railways)** and SNCF connect **Luxembourg City** with Strasbourg in approximately 2 to 2.5 hours. This route is used frequently by business travelers and tourists exploring the broader Grand Est region.

Belgium

Though there are no direct high-speed trains between **Brussels** and Strasbourg, travelers can connect through Paris or Luxembourg. The journey typically takes 4 to 5 hours, depending on transfer time.

Regional Rail Access: TER Grand Est

France's **TER (Transport Express Régional)** trains provide extensive service within the Grand Est region and are ideal for reaching local destinations in Alsace and Lorraine. These trains are slower than TGV but are convenient for short- to medium-distance travel and do not require advance booking.

Notable regional routes:

- **Colmar:** ~30 minutes
- **Mulhouse:** ~1 hour
- **Nancy:** ~1 hour 40 minutes
- **Metz:** ~2 hours
- **Saverne and Haguenau:** 30–45 minutes

TER tickets are affordably priced and can be purchased at machines or online on the day of travel.

Tickets, Reservations, and Travel Classes

- **TGV and ICE:** Seat reservations are mandatory; tickets are subject to dynamic pricing.
- **TER trains:** No seat reservation required; tickets valid for the day of purchase.
- **Booking platforms:** Recommended options include **SNCF Connect**, **Trainline**, **Oui.sncf**, and **Deutsche Bahn** for international routes.
- **Classes:** Most long-distance trains offer second and first-class options. First class typically provides wider seats, more space, power outlets, and quieter compartments.

Luggage and Onboard Services

- Passengers are responsible for their own luggage; no check-in service is provided.
- Overhead racks and dedicated luggage areas are available onboard.
- Amenities on TGV and ICE trains often include:
  - Power outlets (especially in first class)
  - Free Wi-Fi (on select routes)
  - Onboard cafés or snack trolleys
  - Family-friendly and quiet zones

Practical Tips for Train Travelers

- **Arrival Time:** Aim to arrive 15–20 minutes before departure, especially for TGV and international services.

- **Ticket Validation:** Regional (TER) tickets must be validated at yellow machines before boarding; this does not apply to digital or high-speed tickets.
- **Language:** Staff at major stations often speak English and German, in addition to French.
- **Rail Passes:** Consider a **Eurail Pass** or **France Rail Pass** for multiple train journeys across regions or countries.

Conclusion

Traveling to Strasbourg by train is not only practical but also highly enjoyable. With high-speed domestic and international connections, a well-equipped central station, and comprehensive regional services, Strasbourg is fully accessible by rail. Whether you are arriving from Paris, Frankfurt, Basel, or a nearby Alsatian town, the journey by train offers convenience, comfort, and efficiency that suit a wide range of travel needs.

3.3 By Car: Driving to Strasbourg

Strasbourg's location at the crossroads of Western Europe makes it highly accessible by road. For travelers who value flexibility, independence, and the ability to explore at their own pace, driving to Strasbourg is a practical and rewarding option. Whether approaching from within France or from neighboring countries such as Germany,

Switzerland, or Luxembourg, the city is well-connected by an extensive network of highways and regional roads. In addition to the convenience of direct routes, the journey offers scenic views of the Rhine Valley, the Alsace wine route, and the Vosges foothills.

This section outlines everything a traveler needs to know when considering driving to Strasbourg—covering major routes, road conditions, border policies, toll systems, fuel and rest stops, legal requirements, and key tips for both domestic and international visitors.

Key Road Connections

Strasbourg is serviced by a modern and efficient highway infrastructure, offering seamless connectivity to major European cities. The city lies at the intersection of several national and trans-European corridors:

- **A35 Motorway:** The primary north–south axis in Alsace, connecting Strasbourg with Colmar, Mulhouse, and the Swiss border near Basel. Importantly, this section of the A35 is toll-free.
- **A4 Autoroute:** This major east–west motorway links Strasbourg with Metz, Reims, and ultimately Paris. It is a tolled route and part of the European E50 corridor.
- **German A5 Autobahn:** Located just across the Rhine River, this route connects Strasbourg to Karlsruhe, Frankfurt, and other major cities in Germany.
- **D500 and D1083:** Regional roads offering access to Alsace's interior towns and the famed Route des Vins d'Alsace.

Thanks to these connections, driving times from surrounding cities are efficient and comfortable under normal conditions.

Estimated Driving Distances & Times

Origin City	Distance to Strasbourg	Approximate Driving Time
Paris, France	490 km	4.5–5 hours
Frankfurt, Germany	220 km	2.5 hours
Zurich, Switzerland	220 km	3 hours
Luxembourg City	220 km	2.5 hours
Stuttgart, Germany	150 km	2 hours

Colmar, France	75 km	1 hour

Actual travel times may vary due to weather, traffic congestion, or construction, especially during holiday periods and weekends.

Schengen Border Rules and Documentation

France is a member of the Schengen Area, and Strasbourg lies just minutes from Germany's Baden-Württemberg region. Travelers from other Schengen countries can cross borders freely without regular passport checks. However, it remains mandatory to carry personal identification (passport or national ID), a valid driver's license, vehicle registration, and proof of insurance, as spot checks may occur.

For visitors arriving from outside the EU/Schengen Zone, ensure your visa includes multiple-entry privileges if you intend to drive across national borders during your trip.

Toll Roads in France

French motorways are largely operated as toll roads (**autoroutes à péage**), with the exception of certain regional routes such as the **A35**, which is toll-free throughout the Alsace region. If you are arriving via the **A4** from Paris or the **A31** from Luxembourg, you will pass through toll booths.

Toll Information:

- Toll booths accept cash (euros), most credit and debit cards, and **Télépéage** (automated tag systems).
- Rates depend on vehicle category and distance traveled. A journey from Paris to Strasbourg by car typically costs between €35 and €40 in tolls.
- Travelers may check current toll prices using online calculators such as **Autoroutes.fr** or **ViaMichelin**.

Germany's Autobahns are toll-free for private cars, while Switzerland requires a **motorway vignette** (sticker) for access to its highway system. This can be purchased at border crossings and most petrol stations for around CHF 40.

Fuel Availability and Costs

Fuel stations are widely available on motorways and within urban areas. In rural locations, especially late at night or on Sundays, stations may operate on a self-service basis using automated machines that accept international cards or local debit cards.

Fuel Types in France:

- **SP95 / SP98**: Unleaded petrol
- **Gazole**: Diesel
- **E10**: Ethanol-blended fuel (not compatible with all vehicles)

Fuel prices in France tend to be higher than in Germany or Luxembourg. Planning fuel stops strategically before entering France may offer savings.

Parking in Strasbourg

Parking in Strasbourg's historic center can be limited and costly. The city promotes a sustainable transport model, encouraging the use of its extensive public transport network. If arriving by car, consider the following:

- **Park & Ride (P+R):** Strasbourg offers several peripheral parking lots connected to trams and buses. These are cost-effective and allow you to avoid driving into the compact city center.
- **Underground Garages:** Located in areas like Place Kléber, Les Halles, and Gare Centrale, these are secure but priced at a premium.
- **Street Parking:** Metered and regulated, with time limits and higher fees in central zones. Always check signage to avoid fines.

For extended stays, accommodations with on-site parking or private garage rental may offer greater convenience.

Driving Rules and Road Safety

France maintains high road safety standards, and traffic regulations are strictly enforced. Key regulations include:

- **Right-hand driving** with overtaking on the left
- **Seat belts mandatory** for all passengers
- **Mobile phone use prohibited** unless via hands-free systems
- **Blood alcohol limit** of 0.05% (0.02% for novice drivers)
- **Speed Limits:**
  - 50 km/h in urban areas
  - 80–90 km/h on rural roads
  - 110 km/h on dual carriageways
  - 130 km/h on motorways (reduced during rain or poor visibility)

It is also mandatory to carry:

- A reflective safety vest
- Warning triangle
- Breathalyzer kit (not always enforced but recommended)
- Spare bulb kit and fuses (for some rental companies)

Failure to comply may result in on-the-spot fines.

For International Drivers

Visitors from EU and EEA countries can drive in France using their domestic driver's license. Non-EU travelers are typically required to carry an **International Driving Permit (IDP)** in addition to their home country's license. Rental companies may also request an IDP depending on the vehicle class and rental duration.

Ensure your car insurance provides coverage in France. If driving a rented vehicle across borders, inform the rental company in advance and confirm cross-border travel is permitted under your agreement.

Final Considerations

Driving to Strasbourg offers an enriching way to discover both the city and the greater Alsace region. The ability to stop at vineyards, small villages, and regional parks en route adds a depth of experience not available via air or train. That said, it's important to be well-prepared, observe local driving laws, and plan parking or drop-off logistics in advance. For those seeking both convenience and freedom, Strasbourg is unquestionably road-trip friendly.

3.4 By Bus or River Cruise

Strasbourg is exceptionally well-connected, offering travelers multiple ways to arrive with ease—whether by land, air, or water. While most visitors arrive by train or plane, long-distance bus services and river cruises present two distinctive and worthwhile alternatives. These methods not only offer practical benefits like cost savings or scenic value, but they also provide unique entry points into the heart of Alsace—allowing visitors to begin their journey with a memorable view or a comfortable ride through the countryside.

In this section, we'll take a closer look at arriving in Strasbourg via intercity bus or by river cruise—highlighting the major providers, routes, facilities, and travel tips to help you make the most of your journey.

Arriving by Long-Distance Bus

Long-distance buses have seen a rise in popularity across Europe over the past decade. Affordable pricing, extensive networks, and improved onboard comfort have made bus travel a strong alternative to trains—especially for budget travelers and those looking for flexible travel schedules. Strasbourg benefits from its central location near the borders of Germany, Luxembourg, and Switzerland, placing it on major trans-European bus routes.

Several well-known international and regional companies operate services into the city. FlixBus, for instance, is the leading long-distance bus provider in Europe, offering direct connections to and from major cities such as Paris, Frankfurt, Munich, Brussels, Amsterdam, and Zurich. BlaBlaCar Bus, another key player in France, provides frequent domestic routes linking Strasbourg with other French cities, while some seasonal or less frequent lines from operators like Eurolines or RegioJet connect Strasbourg to parts of Central and Southern Europe.

Most of these buses arrive at the Strasbourg Bus Station near Place des Halles, just a short walk or tram ride from the city's central train station (Gare de Strasbourg). The facilities here are basic yet functional—passengers can access ticket kiosks, nearby restrooms, and local food options. From this hub, travelers can easily connect to trams or local buses that run throughout the city.

Choosing to arrive by bus has a few distinct advantages. Firstly, it's usually the most economical option—especially when booked in advance. Second, the routes are often direct, making it an efficient way to reach Strasbourg from nearby European capitals. Buses also tend to have generous baggage allowances compared to budget airlines, and many companies have adopted eco-conscious policies, making them one of the greener travel choices in Europe.

For those who don't mind longer travel times and value affordability and accessibility, long-distance buses are a smart and dependable choice.

Arriving by River Cruise

Strasbourg is not only a city of bridges and canals—it's also an important stop on one of Europe's most iconic rivers: the Rhine. Arriving by river cruise offers an entirely different introduction to the city—one that unfolds gradually as the vessel glides through vineyards, forests, and medieval villages before approaching Strasbourg's charming waterfront.

The city is a highlight on many Rhine cruise itineraries, particularly those traveling between Amsterdam and Basel. Several leading cruise operators include Strasbourg in their routes. Viking River Cruises, AmaWaterways, Scenic Cruises, Tauck, and CroisiEurope (which is based in Strasbourg itself) all offer elegant multi-day voyages along the Rhine, with Strasbourg typically featured as a key cultural stop.

Most river cruise ships dock at the Port Autonome de Strasbourg, located a short distance from the city center. Some smaller ships or specialty cruises may use docking points closer to the Quai des Pêcheurs or near the Orangerie district, especially those operating along the Ill River that surrounds the city's historic center. Cruise companies usually provide transfers from the dock to key landmarks or offer walking tours into town. If you prefer to explore independently, taxis and public transport are readily available from most mooring points, and in many cases, the walk into town is pleasant and manageable.

One of the most attractive features of arriving by river is the level of comfort and convenience. Modern river cruise ships are designed with luxury in mind—offering well-appointed cabins, onboard dining, cultural enrichment programs, and often all-inclusive packages. Many cruises are seasonal, running from April to October, although Strasbourg's world-famous Christmas Market ensures that some winter itineraries are also available.

It's worth noting that while river cruises are significantly more expensive than bus travel, they cater to travelers seeking a more relaxed pace, guided excursions, and a deeper cultural engagement. These voyages are ideal for those who want their journey to be part of the experience—not just a means to get from point A to B.

Final Thoughts

Whether you're rolling into Strasbourg aboard a modern coach from Brussels or sailing into the city on a glassy stretch of the Rhine, both modes of arrival offer something valuable. Long-distance buses are practical, budget-friendly, and flexible. River cruises, meanwhile, provide a scenic and luxurious entry into the city, where every bend of the river feels like a prelude to discovery.

Choosing between them depends on your travel style. If you value convenience, affordability, and straightforward transport, buses are an excellent fit. If you're drawn to leisurely exploration, cultural programming, and a more immersive arrival, a river cruise is well worth considering.

Both options reflect the diversity of Strasbourg's connections—not just geographically, but culturally. Whether by road or water, your journey into the city sets the tone for everything that follows.

Chapter 4: Getting Around Strasbourg

4.1 Public Transportation (Trams, Buses)

Strasbourg boasts one of the most efficient and environmentally forward-thinking public transportation systems in France. Seamlessly blending modern infrastructure with a commitment to sustainability, the city's network of trams and buses provides both residents and visitors with a reliable, affordable, and easy way to move around town and beyond.

For travelers, using public transit isn't just a matter of convenience—it's part of the Strasbourg experience. Whether gliding through the UNESCO-listed Grande Île aboard a sleek tram or hopping on a clean-energy bus to a neighborhood café, the city's transportation system helps you move like a local while reducing your carbon footprint.

Let's take a closer look at how to use Strasbourg's trams and buses effectively—covering routes, tickets, schedules, and insider tips to ensure a smooth journey.

The CTS Network: An Overview

Public transportation in Strasbourg is managed by the CTS (Compagnie des Transports Strasbourgeois), which oversees an integrated system of **tram lines, bus routes, and park-and-ride services** that cover the city center, suburbs, and key points of interest.

The tram system, in particular, has become an iconic part of the city. Known for its quiet operation and sleek design, it stretches across **six main lines (A through F)** and connects neighborhoods, commercial areas, university campuses, and cultural sites. Trams operate frequently and punctually, with service typically starting around **4:30 AM and running until midnight**, extended slightly on weekends.

Buses supplement the tram system by covering areas that trams do not reach—especially the outer districts, nearby villages, and late-night routes. With dozens of lines, including **feeder buses to tram hubs**, the bus network ensures full coverage across the Strasbourg Eurométropole area.

Together, the tram and bus systems provide an exceptionally user-friendly way to explore the city without the stress of driving or the hassle of parking.

Tram Travel: Efficient and Eco-Friendly

Strasbourg's trams are widely considered among the best in Europe—not just for their punctuality, but also for their environmental impact. Nearly all of the power used by the system is renewable, and the city has worked hard to ensure that team development has preserved the character of the historic city center.

The main tram lines include:

- **Line A & D** – Serving the main railway station, Place de l'Étoile, and cross-border stops into Germany (Line D extends to Kehl).
- **Line B & F** – Ideal for reaching universities, the European Parliament, and cultural institutions.
- **Line C & E** – Running through key commercial zones and residential areas.

Each tram is wheelchair accessible, has dedicated space for strollers and bikes during off-peak hours, and is equipped with real-time display screens and audio announcements.

Trams run every **5 to 10 minutes** during peak times, and less frequently in the early morning or late evening. During major events or festivals—such as the Christmas Market—the city often increases frequency or adds additional services.

Bus Travel: Filling in the Gaps

Strasbourg's bus network complements the tram lines by covering destinations not served by rail. While buses may be slightly slower due to traffic, they remain reliable and are especially useful for:

- Reaching **residential zones** outside the tram loop
- Getting to **early morning flights or trains**
- Visiting local villages or the wine road area
- Late-night transport (select **"Noctis" night bus routes** operate on weekends)

Buses are clean, modern, and typically operate from around **5:00 AM to 11:30 PM**, with night services extending into the early hours on Fridays and Saturdays.

Real-time bus information is displayed at many stops, and mobile apps make it easy to track your next arrival.

Tickets, Passes, and Validation

CTS offers a unified fare system that applies to both buses and trams, making transfers between the two seamless. Tickets can be purchased in several convenient ways:

- **Ticket machines** at tram stops (accept cards and coins)
- **CTS mobile app** (for digital tickets and passes)
- **Onboard buses** (contactless payment or coin fare, exact change required)
- **Tabacs and convenience stores** marked with the CTS logo

Common ticket types include:

- **Single ticket** (valid for 1 hour, unlimited transfers)
- **24-hour pass** (unlimited travel for a full day)
- **Group ticket** (for up to three people traveling together)
- **Multi-trip cards** (e.g., 10-trip pack for savings)
- **Tourist pass** (offered seasonally, often includes museum or attraction discounts)

All tickets must be **validated upon boarding**. For trams, this means using the yellow machines on the platform before entering. For buses, use the onboard validator. Fines apply for unvalidated or expired tickets, so be sure to double-check before riding.

Accessibility and Travel Tips

Strasbourg has made strong efforts to ensure its transport system is inclusive and easy to navigate:

- **Wheelchair access** is available on all trams and most buses.
- **Visual and audio signage** helps travelers with hearing or vision impairments.
- **Bike-tram combinations** are possible, though bicycles are allowed only during off-peak hours (usually outside 7–9 AM and 4–6 PM on weekdays).

Here are a few helpful tips for a smooth transit experience:

- **Avoid peak hours** (especially 7:30–9:00 AM and 5:00–6:30 PM) if you're looking for a more relaxed ride.
- **Download the CTS app** for real-time schedules, digital tickets, and trip planning tools.
- **Look for signs marked "Tram en Commun"** when transferring between modes or using Park-and-Ride services.
- **Be aware of strike days**, which occasionally affect transport in France. CTS updates its services regularly via social media and on its website during such times.

Final Thoughts

Whether you're commuting from your hotel to the European Parliament, heading out to explore the Orangerie, or returning late from a riverside dinner in Petite France, Strasbourg's public transportation system makes it easy, efficient, and enjoyable. Clean, safe, and beautifully integrated into the city's fabric, the network not only enhances mobility but also reflects Strasbourg's forward-thinking approach to urban living.

As a visitor, embracing the tram-and-bus system is more than practical—it's one of the best ways to engage with the rhythm and spirit of the city.

4.2 Walking & Cycling in the City

Strasbourg is often described as one of the most walkable and bike-friendly cities in Europe. With its compact city center, extensive pedestrian zones, and a well-developed network of cycle paths, getting around on foot or by bicycle isn't just possible—it's a deeply enjoyable way to explore the city's rich history, charming neighborhoods, and scenic waterfronts.

Whether you're strolling through cobbled alleys in Petite France or pedaling past the European Parliament along the Ill River, moving through Strasbourg on your own two feet—or wheels—offers a level of intimacy and connection with the city that public transit can't replicate. For both short visits and longer stays, walking and cycling are highly recommended as primary modes of transport.

Exploring Strasbourg on Foot

Strasbourg's historic core, known as the **Grande Île**, is a UNESCO World Heritage Site, and much of it is pedestrian-only or heavily restricted to vehicle traffic. This urban design makes walking not only practical but incredibly pleasant. Visitors will find that many of the city's most iconic sites are within easy reach of one another, allowing for spontaneous detours into markets, bakeries, and courtyards without the need to consult a transit map.

Key Walking Areas:

- **Petite France:** Perhaps the most picturesque district in the city, with half-timbered houses, stone bridges, and quiet canals that are best appreciated on foot.
- **Cathédrale Notre-Dame Area:** The area around the cathedral is largely pedestrianized and filled with cafés, boutiques, and historical landmarks.
- **Place Kléber to Place de la République:** A central axis of shopping, culture, and government buildings—ideal for a slow-paced stroll.

Benefits of Walking in Strasbourg:

- **Proximity:** Most major attractions are within a 15- to 25-minute walk of each other.
- **Safety:** Pedestrian areas are clearly marked, well-lit, and well-maintained, even at night.
- **Accessibility:** Sidewalks are wide, crossings are well-signalized, and most areas accommodate wheelchairs and strollers.
- **Ambience:** Street musicians, outdoor art, fountains, and seasonal decorations (especially during the Christmas market) make the walk feel lively and immersive.

Tip: Wear comfortable shoes. While most walking routes are flat, many streets in the old city are paved with cobblestones, which can be uneven or slippery in the rain.

Cycling in Strasbourg: A Model for Urban Mobility

Strasbourg is widely recognized as the **cycling capital of France** and ranks among Europe's top bike-friendly cities. Its cycling infrastructure is vast and continuously expanding, with over **600 kilometers (approx. 370 miles) of bike lanes** threading through the city and its surrounding suburbs.

Cyclists are a common sight in every part of Strasbourg—from professionals commuting to work to students heading to class and tourists enjoying riverside paths. Thanks to thoughtful urban planning, cycling is safe, convenient, and often faster than taking a car or bus for short to medium distances.

Highlights of Strasbourg's Cycling Network:

- **The Pistes Cyclables:** Dedicated bike lanes separated from traffic, running along major boulevards and through quieter neighborhoods.
- **The Canal & River Routes:** Especially popular for leisure cycling, these scenic paths run along the Ill River, the Canal de la Bruche, and other waterways.
- **Green Belt Loops:** The city offers several circular routes that combine urban cycling with rural views, ideal for longer day rides or weekend explorations.
- **Cross-Border Cycling:** You can cycle from Strasbourg to nearby towns in Germany, including Kehl, using dedicated bike bridges and border-friendly lanes.

Bike Rentals & Sharing Systems

For visitors, Strasbourg offers multiple convenient options to rent a bike or use bike-sharing services.

Popular Options Include:

- **Vélhop** – The city's official bike-sharing scheme offers short- and long-term rentals with over 20 automated stations. Bicycles are well-maintained, affordable, and easy to access using the mobile app or card system. Vélhop bikes are ideal for short rides or day-long explorations.
- **Private Rental Shops** – Several rental stores, particularly near the train station and city center, offer road bikes, electric bikes, tandems, and even child seats for families. Rentals can usually be arranged by the hour, day, or week.
- **Hotel & Hostel Bikes** – Many accommodations offer complimentary or discounted bike rentals for guests.

Tip: Helmets are not legally required for adults in France, but it's strongly recommended, especially if you're not used to cycling in urban traffic.

Cycling Etiquette & Safety Guidelines

Strasbourg's residents take cycling seriously, and the city has developed a mature cycling culture. As a visitor, it's important to observe a few key practices to ensure safety and avoid fines:

- **Stay in designated bike lanes** wherever possible.
- **Use hand signals** to indicate turns or stops.
- **Do not cycle on sidewalks** unless explicitly allowed.
- **Obey traffic signals**, especially at intersections shared with vehicles or pedestrians.
- **Use bike lights** after dark (required by law).

- **Lock your bike securely**—bike theft, while not rampant, does occur in busy areas.

Bikes can also be brought onto trams during off-peak hours, though space is limited. Always check signage before boarding.

Combining Walking & Cycling

Many visitors find the best way to explore Strasbourg is through a combination of walking and cycling. For example, you might choose to cycle out to the **Parc de l'Orangerie** or **European Parliament**, lock your bike, and then continue your visit on foot through adjoining gardens and trails.

The city's compact layout, clear signage, and numerous **bike racks, pedestrian zones, and greenways** make transitions between walking and cycling smooth and intuitive.

Final Thoughts

Whether you're an avid cyclist or someone who prefers a relaxed stroll, Strasbourg is uniquely suited to slow and personal forms of travel. Few cities offer such a harmonious balance between modern mobility and preserved history. On foot or by bike, you'll encounter Strasbourg's true rhythm—its quiet corners, friendly residents, hidden cafés, and beautiful surprises that aren't listed on any map.

In Strasbourg, walking and cycling aren't just options—they're invitations to experience the city more fully.

4.3 Car Rentals & Parking

While Strasbourg is best explored on foot or by bike, there are situations where renting a car becomes practical—especially if your itinerary includes excursions into the Alsace countryside, visits to nearby vineyards, or day trips to towns not well served by public transportation. That said, driving in the city center is not always convenient, and parking comes with its own set of considerations. Knowing when and how to rent a car, where to park, and the local traffic norms can make your time in Strasbourg smoother and less stressful.

Do You Really Need a Car in Strasbourg?

Before committing to a rental, it's worth asking whether you truly need one. The city's historic center—the Grande Île—is largely pedestrianized, and the public transport network is extensive and efficient. For most visitors who plan to stay within Strasbourg or venture only short distances by train or tram, a car is unnecessary.

A rental car becomes more useful in the following scenarios:

- You're planning to visit remote villages, wine routes, or mountain areas not covered by rail or bus.
- You're traveling with children or elderly family members and want the convenience of door-to-door transport.
- Your itinerary includes multiple stops across Alsace in a single day.

- You're heading to Germany or other cross-border destinations with rural segments.

Where to Rent a Car in Strasbourg

Strasbourg offers a variety of car rental providers, both international and local, with pick-up locations that are easy to reach.

Major Rental Locations:

- **Strasbourg Airport (SXB):** A convenient choice if you're flying in, with several well-known companies including Avis, Europcar, Hertz, Sixt, and Enterprise. Pick-up desks are located in the arrivals area.
- **Strasbourg Train Station (Gare de Strasbourg-Ville):** Many agencies maintain branches here, making it a practical location if you're arriving by train and want to start your road trip immediately.
- **Downtown Strasbourg:** Additional rental offices can be found around Place Kléber, Rue du Faubourg de Saverne, and Boulevard de Metz. These are ideal for travelers already in the city who want to rent for a day or two.

Rental Tips:

- **Book in advance**, especially in summer or during major holidays like the Christmas market season.
- **Automatic transmissions** are less common and usually more expensive—reserve ahead if you require one.
- Most companies require renters to be at least **21 years old**, though some may charge a surcharge for drivers under 25.
- A **valid driver's license** from your home country is sufficient for most visitors. Non-EU travelers may benefit from carrying an **International Driving Permit (IDP)**, especially when crossing borders or in case of traffic stops.

Driving in Strasbourg: What to Know

Driving in Strasbourg comes with a learning curve, especially for those unfamiliar with European city layouts.

Traffic Regulations:

- **Right-of-way rules** differ slightly from those in North America or Asia; priority is often given to the right at unmarked intersections.
- **Speed limits** are strictly enforced: typically 50 km/h (31 mph) in urban areas, unless otherwise marked.

- The use of **mobile phones** while driving is prohibited unless you have a hands-free device.
- **Roundabouts** are common—always yield to traffic already in the circle.

Environmental Zones:

Strasbourg is part of France's Crit'Air emissions zone. To drive within the city center during pollution alerts or designated low-emission days, your vehicle must display a valid Crit'Air vignette (sticker). Most rental cars are already compliant, but double-check with your agency.

Where to Park in Strasbourg

Parking in Strasbourg, particularly in and around the historic core, can be a challenge if you're unfamiliar with the options. Street parking is available, but often limited or metered. Fortunately, the city offers a well-organized system of parking lots and garages, including **Park & Ride (P+R) facilities** designed to encourage visitors to leave their vehicles outside the city and use public transport.

Parking Options:

- **Street Parking:** Available in most neighborhoods, with varying rates depending on the zone. Paid hours usually apply from Monday to Saturday, 9:00 a.m. to 7:00 p.m. Payment is typically done via parking meters or mobile apps.
- **Underground Garages:** Safe and widely used, especially near Place Kléber, Homme de Fer, and the train station. These are more expensive but offer 24-hour access and better security.
- **Park & Ride (P+R) Facilities:** These are an excellent option for day visitors. Located on the city's outskirts (e.g., Rotonde, Elsau, Baggersee), P+R garages offer affordable daily rates that **include tram tickets for all passengers**. Simply park your car, hop on a tram, and arrive downtown in 10–15 minutes.

Pricing Guide (subject to change):

- **Street parking:** Around €2–€3 per hour in central zones.
- **Underground parking garages:** Approximately €20–€25 for a full day.
- **P+R lots:** Roughly €4.20 per day, including tram access.

Tip: Avoid driving into the Grande Île unless absolutely necessary. Many streets are **pedestrian-only**, and vehicle access is often restricted or requires special permits.

Fuel & Tolls

- **Fuel Stations:** Easily found around the city and along major highways. Prices may vary, with supermarkets like Leclerc or Auchan often offering lower rates.
- **Toll Roads:** Most of Alsace's highways are toll-free, but if you're driving further into France or to Switzerland, expect to pay tolls. Cards and cash are accepted.

Electric Vehicle (EV) Rentals & Charging

Strasbourg is increasingly embracing electric mobility. Several rental companies offer **electric or hybrid vehicles**, especially at the airport and train station.

- **Charging Points:** The city has a growing number of public EV chargers, especially in underground car parks, shopping centers, and municipal lots. Apps like Chargemap or Plugsurfing can help locate nearby stations.
- **Charging Costs:** Typically based on kWh used or flat hourly rates. Always check compatibility and access rules beforehand.

Final Thoughts

Renting a car in Strasbourg is an excellent way to **enhance your freedom of movement**, particularly if your plans include exploring the Alsatian countryside or venturing into nearby regions of Germany and Switzerland. That said, careful planning is essential to avoid the pitfalls of urban traffic and limited parking.

Consider pairing car rental with strategic use of public transport: **rent for a day or two to explore outside the city**, then return to your hotel and enjoy Strasbourg car-free the rest of the time. This balanced approach offers the best of both worlds—freedom to roam and stress-free urban navigation.

4.4 Accessibility Information

Strasbourg has made significant strides in becoming a more inclusive and accessible destination for all travelers. Whether you're navigating the city in a wheelchair, traveling with visual or hearing impairments, or managing mobility limitations, the city offers a range of resources and infrastructure to ensure your visit is comfortable, safe, and enriching.

While challenges remain—particularly in the older quarters like the Grande Île where cobblestones and narrow passageways are common—many public spaces, transportation systems, cultural sites, and accommodations have been adapted to support accessibility. Understanding what to expect before your trip can make planning easier and reduce surprises once you arrive.

Public Transportation Accessibility

Strasbourg's public transit network, operated by CTS (Compagnie des Transports Strasbourgeois), is among the most accessible in France. Both the tram and bus systems have undergone modernization to accommodate passengers with disabilities or reduced mobility.

Trams:

- **Low-floor access:** All tram lines in Strasbourg use low-floor vehicles, making them fully accessible to wheelchairs, walkers, and strollers.
- **Level boarding platforms:** Most stations are designed to be at the same level as the tram floor, enabling easy entry without ramps or assistance.
- **Visual and audio announcements:** Stops are clearly marked with both audio and digital indicators, aiding travelers with hearing or vision impairments.
- **Reserved spaces:** Each tram has dedicated areas for wheelchair users, complete with securing devices.

Buses:

- **Kneeling buses and ramps:** Most city buses are equipped with low-floor technology and manual or automatic ramps.
- **Priority seating:** Seats near the entrance are designated for individuals with reduced mobility, pregnant passengers, and older adults.
- **Service schedules:** While most routes are accessible, it's best to check individual line information or call ahead if traveling during off-peak hours or on less frequent routes.

Train Station Accessibility

Strasbourg's central train station (Gare de Strasbourg-Ville) is a regional and international hub, and it's equipped with accessibility features that support seamless travel.

- **Elevators and escalators:** Provide access between platforms and main hall areas.
- **Tactile paving:** Installed throughout the station to guide visually impaired travelers.
- **Dedicated assistance service (Accès Plus):** Offers help with boarding, disembarking, and navigating the station. Requests must be made at least 48 hours in advance.
- **Accessible restrooms:** Available in the station, with clear signage.
- **Accessible taxis and car pick-up points:** Located just outside the main entrance.

Air Travel and Strasbourg Airport (SXB)

Strasbourg Airport provides basic accessibility infrastructure to accommodate travelers with limited mobility or sensory impairments.

- **Dedicated assistance staff:** Available upon request, from check-in through boarding. Requests should be made via your airline or travel agency at least 48 hours prior to travel.
- **Wheelchair-friendly entrances and elevators:** Throughout the terminal.
- **Priority security lanes:** Often offered to passengers with disabilities to ease the screening process.
- **Accessible restrooms and signage:** Clearly marked and available across the terminal.

Sidewalks and Streets

Strasbourg's historic charm lies in its old streets and medieval architecture, which can sometimes pose obstacles for visitors with mobility challenges. That said, the city has made considerable efforts to modernize infrastructure without compromising its character.

- **Paved sidewalks and curb ramps:** Most central streets, especially in newer districts like Neustadt and around the train station, feature wide sidewalks and lowered curbs at crossings.
- **Challenges in the Grande Île:** Some streets remain cobbled and uneven, which may be difficult to navigate in a wheelchair or with limited balance. Assistance or caution is advised in areas around the Cathedral and Petite France.
- **Pedestrian zones:** Large areas of the city center are pedestrian-only, making them quieter and safer for slower-moving travelers.

Museums and Tourist Attractions

Many of Strasbourg's major attractions are partially or fully accessible, although levels of access can vary depending on the building's age and modifications.

- **Strasbourg Cathedral:** Entry into the nave is step-free, but the viewing platform and upper levels are only accessible via stairs.
- **Palais Rohan Museums (Fine Arts, Decorative Arts, Archaeology):** The museums are located in a historical palace, and accessibility is limited in some wings. Elevators and accessible entrances are present but may require assistance or staff notification.

- **Alsatian Museum:** Due to the building's age and structure, accessibility is limited. Alternative interpretive options are sometimes available upon request.
- **European Parliament and Council of Europe:** Fully accessible, with wheelchair entry, audio guides, and guided tours adapted for visitors with special needs.
- **Boat Tours (Batorama):** Certain boats are wheelchair-accessible, but it's essential to confirm availability and reserve in advance.

Hotels and Accommodation

Strasbourg offers a wide selection of accommodations that cater to travelers with specific accessibility requirements. When booking, it is always advisable to directly confirm the hotel's features, even if it's listed as "accessible."

Look for hotels that offer:

- Step-free entrances and wide doorways
- Elevator access to all floors
- Roll-in showers or shower chairs
- Accessible breakfast rooms or restaurants
- Visual fire alarms and vibrating pillows (for those with hearing impairments)

Some well-rated accessible hotels in central Strasbourg include:

- Hôtel Hannong
- Hôtel Régent Contades
- Holiday Inn Express Strasbourg Centre
- Ibis Strasbourg Centre Petite France

Accessible Toilets and Facilities in Public Areas

Public restrooms adapted for wheelchair users are found in:

- Train stations
- Large shopping centers
- Underground parking garages
- Main tourist zones such as Place Kléber and Parc de l'Orangerie

A useful app such as WheelMate or Jaccede can help locate the nearest accessible toilet or public space based on your location.

Support Services and Resources

Travelers with disabilities can benefit from local organizations and platforms that provide information, advocacy, or hands-on assistance.

- **Tourism Office Services:** Strasbourg's Tourist Office offers brochures in braille, guided tours adapted for all needs, and staff trained to assist travelers with questions related to accessibility.
- **Handicap International France:** While not specific to Strasbourg, this national organization offers guidance and resources for disabled travelers.
- **City of Strasbourg Accessibility Portal:** Updated details on ongoing urban improvements and current accessible facilities.

Practical Tips

- **Plan routes ahead:** Not all historical streets are easy to access, so map out your path to avoid tough terrain.
- **Request assistance early:** Whether at the airport or train station, notify your provider in advance to guarantee help will be available.
- **Use mobile apps:** Apps such as Google Maps (wheelchair-accessible route filter), Accès Plus, and Wheelmap can be helpful in navigating.
- **Travel insurance:** Ensure your insurance covers mobility equipment and potential accessibility-related delays or disruptions.

Conclusion

Strasbourg continues to improve its accessibility infrastructure, aiming to offer a welcoming environment to all travelers, regardless of physical ability. With thoughtful planning and awareness of available services, the city can be both enjoyable and manageable for visitors with special mobility or sensory needs. Whether you're exploring cultural landmarks, taking in the scenery by tram, or strolling through the Christmas markets, Strasbourg strives to ensure that your journey is inclusive, dignified, and memorable.

Chapter 5: Top Attractions in Strasbourg

5.1 Strasbourg Cathedral (Cathédrale Notre-Dame)

Strasbourg Cathedral, officially known as the Cathédrale Notre-Dame de Strasbourg, is the city's most recognizable landmark and one of the crowning architectural achievements of medieval Europe. Standing at 142 meters tall, it held the title of the world's tallest building from 1647 until the late 19th century and still ranks among the tallest churches in the world today. Its prominence dominates the Strasbourg skyline and defines the historic core of the city.

Construction of the cathedral began in 1015, originally in Romanesque style, before the project transitioned into a Gothic vision during the 12th century. Over the course of nearly four centuries, generations of architects, artisans, and masons contributed to the structure's completion, making it a living record of evolving European styles and ecclesiastical ambition. Built primarily from pink sandstone from the nearby Vosges Mountains, the cathedral's facade shimmers in different hues depending on the angle and intensity of the sun—a feature that captivates visitors at all times of day.

Beyond its architectural grandeur, the cathedral serves as a functioning house of worship, a cultural landmark, and a focal point of civic identity. From its intricate carvings and massive rose window to the famous astronomical clock and panoramic city views from the tower platform, every corner of the cathedral reveals centuries of artistry, faith, and resilience.

Location

The Strasbourg Cathedral is centrally located on Place de la Cathédrale in the heart of the Grande Île, Strasbourg's historic island district. This UNESCO World Heritage Site is easily accessible on foot and is surrounded by cafés, shops, and key historical buildings. The cathedral's physical coordinates place it at 48.5817° North, 7.7508° East.

Opening Hours

The interior of the cathedral is generally open to visitors Monday through Saturday from 8:30 AM to 11:15 AM and again from 12:45 PM to 5:45 PM. On Sundays, the cathedral opens in the afternoon from 1:00 PM to 5:30 PM to allow for uninterrupted morning worship. Visitors wishing to view the astronomical clock presentation can enter daily around 11:30 AM, as the multimedia presentation begins shortly before noon.

Access to the cathedral's viewing platform—via a 332-step spiral staircase—is available from April to September between 9:30 AM and 8:00 PM, and from October to March between 10:00 AM and 5:30 PM. Final admission is typically allowed 30 minutes before closing. It is advised to check ahead during religious holidays, special events, or adverse weather conditions, which may affect access to certain areas.

Admission Fees

Entry into the cathedral's main nave and interior is free of charge. However, access to certain features comes with a modest admission fee. Visitors wishing to attend the astronomical clock's noon presentation can expect to pay approximately €3 for adults and €2 for students and seniors. Children under six years of age are usually admitted free. Access to the tower viewing platform requires a separate ticket, priced at around €8 for adults and €5 for students or job seekers. These prices are subject to change and may vary depending on season and visitor category.

Official Website

For current information on opening hours, special events, and ticket reservations, visitors are encouraged to consult the cathedral's official website:
www.cathedrale-strasbourg.fr

The site provides details in French, English, and German.

Key Features

The facade of Strasbourg Cathedral is one of the most detailed and awe-inspiring examples of Gothic stonework in Europe. Hundreds of sculpted figures, arches, and traceries seem to dance across its towering surface. The west front, with its single 142-meter-high spire, exemplifies the vertical dynamism characteristic of High Gothic design. It is an unparalleled expression of religious devotion, technical prowess, and artistic finesse.

Inside, visitors are often struck by the quality and size of the stained-glass windows, many of which date back to the 12th through 14th centuries. These panels depict stories from the Bible, saints, and civic figures of the medieval city. The light that filters through them fills the cavernous interior with color and atmosphere, creating a sense of reverence and timelessness.

One of the most famous features of the cathedral is the astronomical clock, a Renaissance-era mechanical masterpiece standing 18 meters high. Designed in the 16th century and later restored, the clock tracks the positions of the sun and moon, displays the date and time, and presents a remarkable daily show featuring animated apostles, a crowing rooster, and symbolic figures representing the stages of life. The presentation begins around 11:35 AM, with the full animated sequence unfolding at noon.

Those who are able to climb the cathedral tower are rewarded with sweeping views of Strasbourg's old town, the River Ill, the Black Forest across the German border, and, on clear days, the distant Vosges Mountains. The ascent of 332 stone steps is a challenge, but the panoramic reward is well worth the effort.

Another standout feature is the suspended Great Organ, dating from the 14th century, with its elaborately carved and gilded case. It is one of the most historically significant instruments in France and plays a prominent role during religious services and concerts.

Visitor Services

Multilingual guided tours are available through both the Strasbourg Tourist Office and private operators. These tours typically focus on the cathedral's architectural history, religious significance, and its role in Strasbourg's development. Group and private tours can be arranged, and audio guides are available in several languages for independent visitors.

There is a small gift shop near the entrance that offers a range of items including books, postcards, locally crafted souvenirs, and religious artifacts. The surrounding Place de la Cathédrale is also home to numerous bookstores, artisan shops, and traditional Alsatian restaurants.

Photography is permitted inside the cathedral, though visitors are asked to avoid the use of flash or tripods, especially during mass or quiet hours. As a working place of worship, it is important to be respectful of ongoing religious ceremonies.

The cathedral's nave is wheelchair accessible via a designated side entrance. However, the tower platform is not suitable for visitors with mobility issues due to the narrow and steep staircase. Public restrooms are available nearby, particularly around Place Gutenberg and Place du Château.

Tips for Visitors

To make the most of a visit, it is advisable to arrive early in the day, especially during summer months and holiday periods. The cathedral tends to be busiest between late morning and mid-afternoon. Early arrival also allows for better light conditions if photography is a priority.

For a more spiritual and immersive experience, attending a Sunday Mass or one of the cathedral's musical performances can offer a unique perspective on the building's function and acoustics.

Those visiting during the Christmas season should take extra time to explore the exterior lighting displays, special concerts, and festive decor that turn the cathedral into the centerpiece of Strasbourg's world-renowned Christmas markets.

During summer, special evening light shows known as "illumination spectacles" project vibrant colors and historical narratives onto the facade, offering a dramatic new view of the cathedral's architecture after dark.

Nearby Attractions

The cathedral is surrounded by a rich array of cultural and historical landmarks. Just steps away is the Palais Rohan, which houses three of Strasbourg's most prominent museums—the Museum of Fine Arts, the Archaeological Museum, and the Museum of Decorative Arts. The Maison Kammerzell, a beautifully preserved 15th-century timber-framed building, now operates as a popular restaurant and photo stop.

Other nearby sites include the Place Gutenberg, often used for open-air exhibitions and events, and the riverbanks of the Ill, where boat tours offer a relaxing and informative way to appreciate Strasbourg's layout and history.

Conclusion

Strasbourg Cathedral is more than a monument. It is a living testament to the artistic and spiritual ambitions of an era that continues to inspire awe. Whether you are drawn to its architectural splendor, its religious importance, or its cultural resonance, a visit to the cathedral is a highlight of any journey to Strasbourg. Every element—from the stone facade to the clockwork choreography—contributes to a powerful sense of place that defines the city's character and its enduring legacy in European history.

5.2 La Petite France

La Petite France is arguably the most enchanting and iconic neighborhood in Strasbourg. Located on the western end of the Grande Île—the historic city center and UNESCO World Heritage Site—this area is a postcard-perfect maze of narrow cobblestone streets, half-timbered houses, flower-lined canals, and quaint bridges. Once home to fishermen, tanners, and millers during the Middle Ages, La Petite France has evolved into a symbol of Strasbourg's charm and cultural heritage.

Its name, contrary to what some assume, has nothing to do with national identity or patriotism. It originates from a 15th-century hospital located in the area, the "Hospice des Vérolés," which treated soldiers with syphilis, a disease then referred to in German as "Franzosenkrankheit" (French disease). Over time, the entire neighborhood inherited the moniker "La Petite France." Today, the district bears no trace of that dark chapter. Instead, it welcomes visitors with a timeless ambiance and the well-preserved aesthetic of Renaissance Alsace.

The area is crisscrossed by canals of the River Ill, and its characteristic houses with sloping roofs and timber façades reflect beautifully in the water, especially at sunset. With its mix of history, romance, and photogenic architecture, La Petite France is one of the most visited and photographed locations in Strasbourg—and rightly so.

Location

La Petite France is situated at the western edge of the Grande Île, bordered by the River Ill and the Canal du Faux-Rempart. It's just a short walk from Place Kléber, the Strasbourg Cathedral, and the central train station. Visitors typically enter the neighborhood from Rue du Bain-aux-Plantes, one of its most well-known and picturesque streets.

Because it is located within Strasbourg's pedestrian-friendly city center, La Petite France is easily accessible on foot, by tram (nearest stops: Alt Winmärik or Langstross/Grand Rue), or via river cruise tours that pass through its scenic locks.

Opening Hours & Admission

La Petite France is not a single building or museum, but an open district, so it has no official opening hours or entrance fees. The streets, bridges, and waterfronts can be explored freely at any time of day or night. That said, most of the area's restaurants, cafes, museums, and galleries operate between mid-morning and late evening, typically from around 10:00 AM to 10:00 PM.

Visitors interested in taking guided tours or boat rides through La Petite France should refer to the Strasbourg Tourist Office for schedules and fees, which vary depending on the season.

Key Features

Historic Half-Timbered Houses
The most striking feature of La Petite France is its concentration of historic Alsatian homes. These timber-framed buildings date back to the 16th and 17th centuries and showcase the region's vernacular architecture, with steep gabled roofs, exposed wooden

beams, and brightly painted façades. Many still retain their original features, including pulley systems used by tanners to hang hides for drying.

Quai de la Petite France and Rue du Bain-aux-Plantes

These pedestrian streets are the most popular in the area, lined with flower boxes, artisan shops, and inviting cafes. Rue du Bain-aux-Plantes, in particular, is known for its photogenic row of houses that lean slightly toward the canal. It's one of the best places to capture the postcard shot of Strasbourg.

The Ponts Couverts (Covered Bridges)

Though the wooden covers that once protected these bridges from weather are long gone, the Ponts Couverts remain iconic. This sequence of three stone bridges, flanked by four medieval towers, was originally part of the city's fortifications. Today, they offer excellent views of the canals and old town, especially at dawn and dusk.

The Barrage Vauban (Vauban Dam)

Built in the late 17th century as a defensive flood structure, the Barrage Vauban now features a panoramic terrace that provides sweeping views over La Petite France. It's an ideal place for photography, especially during Strasbourg's golden hour when the rooftops and canals are bathed in warm light.

Canals and Locks

La Petite France is interwoven with canals once vital for commerce and industry. Today, these waterways serve a more scenic purpose. Boats from Batorama river cruises navigate through the locks in this district, giving passengers a dynamic view of the area from water level.

Place Benjamin-Zix

This small square is often filled with artists and musicians in the warmer months. It's also a favorite gathering place, with several cafes that offer outdoor seating and unobstructed views of historic façades and the passing boats.

Visitor Services

There are numerous restaurants, bistros, and bakeries within La Petite France offering traditional Alsatian cuisine—think tarte flambée, choucroute garnie, baeckeoffe, and kougelhopf. Many venues cater to tourists but strive to maintain culinary authenticity. Reservations are recommended for dinner, especially on weekends or during peak travel months.

Shops in the district sell handcrafted goods, regional wines, Alsatian pottery, and souvenirs, often showcasing the cross-cultural influence of both French and German heritage. Look for family-run boutiques rather than chain stores for a more authentic experience.

Accommodation options within or near La Petite France range from luxury hotels with river views to smaller guesthouses tucked away in charming alleys. Many buildings have been thoughtfully renovated, offering historic ambiance with modern comforts.

The Strasbourg Tourist Office provides maps and walking guides for the area, and seasonal walking tours are available in multiple languages, often focusing on the architecture, culinary traditions, and historical anecdotes of the neighborhood.

Tips for Visitors

- **Early mornings** offer a peaceful, nearly tourist-free atmosphere, perfect for photography or quiet walks. Evening strolls can also be magical when the canals reflect the glow of streetlamps.
- **Winter visits**, especially in December, allow travelers to see La Petite France dressed in lights and festive decor as part of the Strasbourg Christmas Market—one of the oldest and most atmospheric in Europe.
- **Be mindful of crowds**, particularly from late spring to early autumn, when the narrow alleys can become quite busy.
- **Wear comfortable shoes.** While charming, the cobblestone streets can be uneven and hard on the feet.
- **Avoid rushing.** The beauty of La Petite France lies in its details—lingering over an espresso, watching the boats go by, or admiring the window boxes in bloom.

Nearby Attractions

La Petite France is well-positioned for continuing exploration of Strasbourg's old town. Just a few minutes away on foot are Place Kléber (the city's commercial heart), the Strasbourg Museum of Modern and Contemporary Art, and the Strasbourg Train Station. From here, it's also easy to connect with other city landmarks such as the Strasbourg Cathedral and the Neustadt district.

Conclusion

La Petite France is not just a neighborhood; it's an immersive journey into the soul of Strasbourg. Its canals, timbered houses, and romantic atmosphere tell stories of both daily life and deep history, all wrapped in an aesthetic that feels timeless. Whether you come to take photos, savor a meal, or simply wander without a plan, this district delivers something rare in the modern world: the sense of having stepped into a living storybook.

5.3 European Parliament

The European Parliament in Strasbourg stands as a modern emblem of unity, democracy, and cooperation across the continent. As one of the key institutions of the European Union (EU), it serves as a legislative body with representatives from all 27 member states. Though the European Parliament has three official working locations—Brussels, Luxembourg, and Strasbourg—its official seat is in Strasbourg. This makes the city one of the few places in the world that hosts a major international parliamentary assembly.

Located in the northeastern district of Wacken, along the River Ill, the Louise Weiss building—named after a prominent French journalist and European campaigner—is both a functional center of political decision-making and a striking architectural landmark. Its elliptical glass façade, expansive debating chamber, and environmentally conscious design all reflect the Parliament's modern character and symbolic openness.

For visitors, the European Parliament offers an opportunity to see European politics in action and gain insight into the workings of a transnational institution that affects the lives of over 400 million EU citizens. Whether you're a student of politics, a curious traveler, or simply interested in the future of Europe, the Parliament is one of Strasbourg's most important and thought-provoking sites.

Location

Address:
Allée du Printemps, 67070 Strasbourg, France

Situated northeast of the city center, the European Parliament complex is easily reachable by public transport, bicycle, or car. It's just a few tram stops from Strasbourg's Grande Île, with the closest tram station being **Parlement Européen (Line E)**.

Opening Hours & Admission

- **Opening Hours:**
  Visitors can explore the European Parliament year-round. The Visitors' Center (Parlamentarium Simone Veil) is generally open:
    - Monday to Friday: 9:00 AM – 6:00 PM
    - Saturdays: 9:30 AM – 12:00 PM & 1:00 PM – 5:00 PM
    - Closed on Sundays and EU public holidays
- **Admission:**
  Entry is **free of charge**, but advance booking is strongly recommended—especially for groups and during plenary session weeks when the Parliament is in full operation.
- **Website for Reservations and Information:**
  europarl.europa.eu/visiting

Key Features

Louise Weiss Building
This is the heart of the Strasbourg seat of the Parliament. Opened in 1999, its bold and transparent architecture was designed to reflect democratic values. The vast hemispherical plenary chamber, with seating for 751 Members of the European Parliament (MEPs), is the largest of its kind in Europe.

Plenary Sessions
Strasbourg hosts 12 plenary sessions each year, typically scheduled during one week of each month. These sessions are when major debates and legislative votes take place, and they offer a unique chance to witness the workings of European democracy. Public visitors can observe proceedings from the gallery with prior registration.

Parlamentarium Simone Veil

This modern visitor center includes multilingual interactive exhibits that explain how the EU works, the legislative process, and how policies affect citizens. Touchscreens, multimedia stations, and short films make the information accessible and engaging.

Guided Tours

Individual visitors can take self-guided audio tours or request guided group visits, available in all 24 official EU languages. A typical visit includes the debating chamber, the visitor center, and a brief educational film in the chamber itself.

Art and Architecture

The complex also features significant contemporary art installations and symbolic design elements. The unfinished tower-like structure of the Louise Weiss building has been interpreted as a metaphor for the ever-evolving European project.

Visitor Services

- **Multilingual Materials:** All signage, brochures, and tour content are available in the EU's official languages.
- **Accessibility:** The Parliament is fully wheelchair-accessible and equipped with elevators, adapted restrooms, and assistance upon request.
- **Security:** Visitors must pass through airport-style security screening. ID (passport or national ID card) is required for entry.
- **Cafeteria & Facilities:** A small café and seating area are available, along with cloakrooms and restrooms.
- **Photography:** Allowed in most public areas but restricted during plenary sessions.

Tips for Visitors

- **Check the Plenary Calendar:** If you're hoping to witness a live session, consult the official calendar in advance. Seats can fill up quickly during high-profile debates.
- **Bring Identification:** A valid government-issued ID is mandatory to enter the premises. Without it, access will be denied.
- **Arrive Early:** Expect security screening and registration procedures—especially during busy times or when traveling with a group.
- **Plan for 1–2 Hours:** Allow enough time to fully explore the visitor center and, if possible, catch a glimpse of a live debate or vote.
- **Use Public Transport:** Due to limited parking and occasional security-related closures, taking the tram is the most efficient way to reach the site.

Nearby Attractions

- **Parc de l'Orangerie:** Just across the street, this elegant 18th-century park offers peaceful walking trails, a small zoo, and a charming lake with rowboat rentals.
- **European Court of Human Rights:** Another symbol of European governance, located nearby and often visited in tandem with the Parliament.
- **European Institutions District:** The Parliament is part of a larger complex that includes the Council of Europe and other EU agencies, ideal for those interested in international politics and diplomacy.

Conclusion

The European Parliament in Strasbourg is far more than a glass-and-steel building on the edge of town—it's a working symbol of continental cooperation, democratic values, and the challenges and hopes of a complex union. Whether you attend a live session, browse interactive exhibits, or simply admire the architecture, the Parliament offers visitors a tangible and inspiring look at how Europe's future is being shaped, one vote at a time.

5.4 Palais Rohan

The Palais Rohan is one of Strasbourg's most iconic and culturally significant landmarks, renowned for its classical architecture, artistic treasures, and historical stature. Often referred to as the "Versailles of Alsace," this elegant 18th-century palace was originally built as the residence for the Prince-Bishops and Cardinals of the House of Rohan. Over the centuries, it has hosted emperors, kings, and cultural elites, including Napoleon Bonaparte and King Louis XV.

Today, the Palais Rohan serves as the home to **three major museums**: the Museum of Fine Arts, the Museum of Decorative Arts, and the Archaeological Museum. Each offers a rich window into different periods of European history and artistry—from ancient artifacts to Renaissance masterpieces. Its location, just steps from the Strasbourg Cathedral and overlooking the Ill River, places it at the cultural heart of the city.

A visit to the Palais Rohan is not just a museum tour—it's a journey through Strasbourg's royal, artistic, and civic heritage, all within one architectural jewel.

Location

Address:
2 Place du Château, 67000 Strasbourg, France
  The palace is centrally located next to the Strasbourg Cathedral, making it easily accessible by foot, tram, or bicycle.

Opening Hours & Admission

Opening Hours:

- **Wednesday to Monday:** 10:00 AM – 1:00 PM and 2:00 PM – 6:00 PM
- **Closed on Tuesdays**, as well as January 1st, May 1st, November 1st, and December 25th.

Admission Fees:

- Full price: €7
- Reduced price: €3.50 (students, seniors, etc.)
- Free entry on the **first Sunday of each month** and for individuals under 18, disabled visitors, and job seekers (with ID)

Website for More Information and Tickets:
strasbourg-musees.eu

Key Features

Museum of Fine Arts (Musée des Beaux-Arts)
  Located on the upper floor, this museum houses an exceptional collection of European paintings from the Middle Ages to the 19th century. Expect works by Raphael, Botticelli, El Greco, Rubens, Goya, and Delacroix. It offers a sweeping narrative of European art movements, curated with sophistication and clarity.

Museum of Decorative Arts (Musée des Arts Décoratifs)
  Situated on the ground floor in the former apartments of the cardinals, this museum showcases 18th-century furnishings, porcelain, ceramics, clocks, and goldsmith work. The luxurious Rococo rooms, with original wood paneling, give a glimpse into aristocratic life in the ancien régime.

Archaeological Museum (Musée Archéologique)
  Housed in the basement, this is one of the oldest museums in Strasbourg and focuses

on Alsace's ancient past. The exhibits include Roman mosaics, Merovingian jewelry, and Celtic tools, offering insights into life in the region from prehistory to the early Middle Ages.

Palatial Architecture

Designed by royal architect Joseph Massol, the palace features a harmonious classical layout, grand staircases, symmetrical facades, and rich interior detailing. Its symmetry and stateliness represent French Enlightenment ideals and ecclesiastical prestige.

Visitor Services

- **Multilingual Audio Guides:** Available for a small additional fee, offering insights into key exhibits and architectural features.
- **Gift Shop:** Offers art books, postcards, prints, and locally crafted souvenirs.
- **Restrooms & Lockers:** Available near the entrance.
- **Accessibility:** The ground floor and some exhibits are wheelchair-accessible; however, full access to upper floors may be limited due to the historical structure.
- **Photography:** Non-flash photography is allowed in most sections of the museums; restrictions apply to specific artworks.

Tips for Visitors

- **Plan Ample Time:** Each museum can take up to an hour to explore. Allocate at least 2–3 hours for a comprehensive visit.
- **Start from the Top:** Begin with the Fine Arts Museum upstairs and work your way down to avoid doubling back.
- **Combine with Cathedral Visit:** Its proximity to the Strasbourg Cathedral makes for an easy and enriching half-day cultural itinerary.
- **Bring ID for Discounts:** European students, youth, and seniors can receive reduced entry with valid ID.
- **Use the Audio Guide:** It enhances the historical context and brings the exhibits to life, especially in the Decorative Arts section.

Nearby Attractions

- **Strasbourg Cathedral (Cathédrale Notre-Dame):** Directly next to the palace and perfect to visit before or after.
- **Place du Château:** A lovely square for photos and a moment of rest with nearby cafés.

- **Historical Museum of Strasbourg:** Just a short walk away, offering deeper insight into Strasbourg's civic evolution.

Conclusion

The Palais Rohan is more than a grand residence—it's a cultural time capsule that brings together art, history, and architecture under one magnificent roof. Whether you're admiring the delicate brushstrokes of an Italian master, wandering through opulent 18th-century salons, or exploring the remnants of ancient Alsace, the palace offers an unforgettable encounter with Strasbourg's multifaceted past. For travelers with a love for culture, it's not just a recommended stop—it's essential.

5.5 Parc de l'Orangerie

Parc de l'Orangerie is Strasbourg's oldest and most beloved public park—a harmonious blend of landscaped beauty, leisure activities, and historical charm. Located directly across from the European Parliament in the city's upscale Orangerie district, this expansive green space has served as a recreational haven since the late 17th century. Originally developed under the guidance of André Le Nôtre, the famed landscape architect behind the gardens of Versailles, the park was later expanded during the Napoleonic era and has since become an essential part of local life.

Parc de l'Orangerie offers more than just scenic strolls—it's a multifunctional space perfect for families, couples, joggers, and anyone looking for a moment of calm or recreation. Complete with a small zoo, boating lake, elegant pavilion, and well-maintained gardens, it offers something for every kind of visitor, whether you're stopping by for a picnic, a jog, or a full afternoon of exploration.

Location

Address:
Allée de la Robertsau, 67000 Strasbourg, France

The park lies northeast of the historic center and is easily accessible via tram or on foot. Its central location near European institutions makes it a natural pairing for a visit to the European Quarter.

Opening Hours & Admission

Opening Hours:

- Open daily, year-round
- Summer: 6:30 AM – 10:00 PM
- Winter: 6:30 AM – 8:00 PM

Admission:
Free entry to the park grounds. Some attractions within the park, such as the zoo and boating rentals, may charge modest fees.

Website for Information:
www.strasbourg.eu

Key Features

Landscaped Gardens and Trails
Parc de l'Orangerie is spread over more than 26 hectares, with French-style formal gardens, shaded promenades, expansive lawns, and romantic bridges crossing tranquil streams. Walking paths and bike lanes weave through the park, providing scenic routes for both leisure and exercise.

Boating Lake
A central lake with rental rowboats allows visitors to drift quietly through a peaceful aquatic landscape. It's especially popular in spring and summer when the surrounding flora is in full bloom.

The Pavillon Joséphine

This neoclassical pavilion, built in honor of Empress Joséphine, Napoleon Bonaparte's first wife, serves as a venue for temporary art exhibits and civic events. The elegant building is surrounded by manicured flowerbeds and makes for a lovely photo backdrop.

Small Zoo and Farm

Open year-round and free to the public, the zoo houses regional and exotic species in a family-friendly setting. From flamingos and monkeys to goats and peacocks, it's particularly popular with children.

Playgrounds and Family Spaces

Parc de l'Orangerie is one of the most family-oriented green spaces in Strasbourg. Modern playgrounds, a vintage carousel, picnic areas, and open spaces make it ideal for parents with young children.

Stork Sanctuary

One of the park's most iconic features is its stork enclosure. As the symbol of Alsace, storks have a special place in regional culture. Here, you'll find them nesting in tall trees and rooftops—often visible from the walking paths.

Visitor Services

- **Restrooms:** Public facilities available throughout the park.
- **Picnic Areas:** Designated spots with tables and benches.
- **Boating Rentals:** Seasonal rentals at the lake, typically April through October.
- **Concessions:** Seasonal cafés and refreshment stands near the lake and playgrounds.
- **Event Space:** The Pavillon Joséphine occasionally hosts public exhibitions and cultural events.
- **Parking:** Limited street parking available; public transport is recommended.

Tips for Visitors

- **Ideal in Spring & Summer:** The park is at its most vibrant between April and September, when the flowers are in bloom and boat rentals are available.
- **Bring a Blanket:** Locals often lounge on the lawns on sunny afternoons—feel free to pack a book and join them.
- **Watch for Storks:** Early spring is nesting season, and it's a particularly photogenic time to visit.
- **Perfect for a Half-Day Trip:** Combine your visit with a walk through the European Quarter or a lunch at one of the nearby cafés.

Nearby Attractions

- **European Parliament:** Located just across the street, it offers guided tours and photo opportunities.
- **Avenue de la Robertsau:** A charming boulevard lined with stately mansions and embassies.
- **Place de l'Europe:** A green plaza where the Council of Europe and European Court of Human Rights are located.

Conclusion

Parc de l'Orangerie is more than just a park—it's a reflection of Strasbourg's balance between refinement and everyday charm. With its serene lake, elegant gardens, and family-friendly attractions, it serves as a sanctuary in the midst of city life. Whether you're a traveler seeking a quiet break or a family in search of wholesome recreation, this park offers the perfect setting to pause, relax, and enjoy Strasbourg's gentler rhythms.

Chapter 6: Cultural Highlights & Activities

6.1 Local Festivals and Events

Strasbourg is a city that thrives on tradition, culture, and community—traits most visibly celebrated through its vibrant calendar of festivals and public events. With deep-rooted customs, seasonal celebrations, and internationally renowned cultural showcases, the city offers visitors year-round opportunities to engage with the local spirit. From medieval-inspired street processions to cutting-edge music and art festivals, Strasbourg's events reflect the city's unique position at the crossroads of French and German heritage.

Overview

The city's annual events range from centuries-old traditions, like the famed Christmas market, to modern festivals spotlighting film, music, street art, and gastronomy. Many take place in Strasbourg's picturesque historic center, while others unfold in scenic parks, along the Ill River, or in the sleek European Quarter. Whether you're planning a trip in spring, summer, or during the cozy winter months, there's likely a notable event happening somewhere in the city that will enrich your experience.

Major Annual Events in Strasbourg

Strasbourg Christmas Market (Marché de Noël)

Dates: Late November to December 24
Location: Grande Île and Place Kléber
Widely recognized as one of the oldest and most iconic Christmas markets in Europe, Strasbourg's *Marché de Noël* draws visitors from all over the world. Dating back to 1570, the market transforms the city into a glowing winter wonderland with more than 300 chalets offering local crafts, mulled wine, baked goods, and holiday decorations. The Great Christmas Tree at Place Kléber, the light displays, and the festive concerts create a magical atmosphere that's impossible to overlook. It's one of Strasbourg's proudest cultural assets.

Strasbourg European Fantastic Film Festival (FEFFS)

Dates: Late September to early October
Location: Various cinemas and cultural venues
A leading genre film event in Europe, the *Festival Européen du Film Fantastique de Strasbourg* showcases fantasy, horror, science fiction, and thriller films from around the world. It includes outdoor screenings, panel discussions, and an annual zombie walk through the city—a quirky favorite among locals and tourists alike.

Musica – Contemporary Music Festival

Dates: Late September to early October
Location: Concert halls and churches around Strasbourg
This prestigious festival has become one of France's top showcases for avant-garde and experimental music. With concerts, sound installations, and live performances featuring international composers, *Musica* challenges audiences to rethink sound and space. Classical music lovers and modernists alike find it an unforgettable cultural dive.

St'art – European Contemporary Art Fair

Dates: November
Location: Parc des Expositions
St'art is Strasbourg's flagship contemporary art fair, drawing galleries and collectors from across Europe. It features paintings, photography, sculpture, and mixed media works, with a strong focus on European artistic movements. It's a must for art enthusiasts and cultural travelers.

Strasbourg Mon Amour

Dates: February (around Valentine's Day)
Location: Throughout the city
This romantic winter festival embraces Strasbourg's charm with events like poetry readings, live music, pop-up dinners, river cruises, and dance parties—all designed for couples and lovers of ambiance. It's both whimsical and sophisticated, offering a fresh take on the city in winter.

Summer Outdoor Cinema Series

Dates: July–August
Location: Public parks and squares
When the weather warms up, Strasbourg rolls out a beloved tradition of free open-air film screenings. Held in parks such as Parc de l'Orangerie or Place du Château, the series features a mix of classic French films, international hits, and family-friendly favorites, all projected under the stars.

National Day (Fête Nationale)

Date: July 14
Location: City-wide
France's national holiday is celebrated with great fanfare in Strasbourg. The festivities typically include a military parade, live music, public dances (*bals populaires*), and a grand fireworks show over the Ill River. The event combines patriotism and festive flair in classic Alsatian style.

Additional Seasonal & Local Events

- **Carnaval de Strasbourg (February–March):** A colorful parade with floats, costumes, and street performances celebrating the end of winter.
- **Fête de la Musique (June 21):** Part of the nationwide music celebration, featuring dozens of free concerts across the city—from jazz quartets to DJs and indie rock bands.
- **Journées Européennes du Patrimoine (European Heritage Days – mid-September):** A weekend when many historic sites, private mansions, and government buildings open their doors to the public for free.
- **Night of the Museums (May):** Museums stay open late and offer special exhibits, performances, and guided tours after dark.
- **Strasbourg Jazzdor Festival (November):** An acclaimed festival spotlighting contemporary jazz talents from France, Germany, and beyond.

What to Expect as a Visitor

- **Crowds:** Major events—especially the Christmas market and music festivals—can draw large crowds, so plan accommodations and transport early.
- **Weather Considerations:** Outdoor events depend on weather conditions. Spring and summer festivals are generally safe bets for good weather.
- **Multilingual Programs:** Many events offer bilingual (French and English) signage or programs, though some local performances may be entirely in French or Alsatian dialects.
- **Free & Ticketed Access:** Some events, like public concerts and film nights, are free. Others, particularly art and music festivals, require advance tickets or day passes.
- **Local Engagement:** Many festivals include activities for children and families, workshops, pop-up food stalls, and cultural demonstrations—encouraging full community participation.

Tips for Festival-Goers

- **Book Accommodations Early:** Strasbourg's hotels and guesthouses often reach capacity during major festivals, especially in December and early autumn.
- **Use Public Transport:** Many festivals occur in pedestrian zones. Trams and buses are the best way to get around during peak event periods.
- **Check Official Schedules:** The city's tourism website and festival-specific platforms offer updated details on programming, locations, and ticketing.
- **Dress Appropriately:** Outdoor winter events like the Christmas market require warm clothing. Summer events call for sun protection and hydration.
- **Blend with Locals:** Don't hesitate to join a dance, taste local food at a market stall, or ask locals for event tips—they're usually welcoming and happy to share insights.

Final Thoughts

Strasbourg's cultural calendar is more than a lineup of events—it's a yearlong expression of the city's dynamic character. With deep traditions, creative innovation, and a passion for sharing its heritage, Strasbourg offers something engaging every season. Whether you're drawn by twinkling lights and mulled wine in winter or outdoor concerts and modern art in summer, the city's festivals provide a unique, local way to connect with its soul.

6.2 Theatrical Performances & Music

Strasbourg is more than just picturesque canals and half-timbered facades—it is a city steeped in cultural sophistication, with a rich tradition of live performance. The performing arts scene here bridges classical refinement and contemporary innovation, offering residents and visitors alike a full spectrum of theatrical and musical experiences throughout the year. From grand opera productions and orchestral concerts to experimental theater and intimate jazz clubs, Strasbourg's venues and programming reflect its identity as both a European capital and a deeply Alsatian city.

Whether you're a devotee of Mozart, a theater enthusiast, or someone who simply enjoys a night out immersed in local culture, Strasbourg has something for every artistic taste. Its stages are alive with French, German, and international influences, underscoring the city's position as a historic and contemporary cultural crossroads.

Theater in Strasbourg

Strasbourg has long maintained a vibrant theatrical tradition, with performances available in French, German, and even Alsatian dialects. The city is home to several important institutions, as well as numerous smaller venues that host touring companies, student productions, and experimental performances.

Théâtre National de Strasbourg (TNS)

Located on Place de la République, the TNS is one of France's most prestigious and influential theater institutions. It is the only national theater outside Paris and is renowned for its bold and thought-provoking programming. TNS produces a mix of classical repertoire, contemporary works, and original pieces, frequently directed by some of the most notable names in French theater. The venue also houses the École Supérieure d'Art Dramatique, a national drama school that trains the next generation of performers, directors, and playwrights.

Audiences can expect high production values, politically engaged themes, and a fusion of traditional and experimental techniques. Most performances are in French, but the venue often provides program notes in English and occasionally offers surtitled performances for major productions.

Le Maillon – Théâtre de Strasbourg – Scène Européenne

This contemporary performance venue specializes in cutting-edge theater, dance, and interdisciplinary productions from across Europe. With a mission to challenge conventional artistic boundaries, Le Maillon regularly hosts avant-garde plays, physical theater, and multimedia installations. Located in the rapidly developing Wacken district, it reflects Strasbourg's progressive artistic spirit and European outlook. It is especially popular among younger audiences and fans of modern, non-traditional stage work.

Other Local Theaters

- **Théâtre du PréO (Oberhausbergen):** A smaller venue known for family-friendly productions and local talent.
- **Théâtre Jeune Public (TJP):** Focuses on performances for children and young adults, blending puppetry, storytelling, and visual theater with sophistication that also appeals to adults.
- **L'Éclat and L'Illiade (Illkirch):** Suburban stages that showcase local artists and touring acts, often with a more relaxed atmosphere and community-centered programming.

Music in Strasbourg

Strasbourg's music scene is just as diverse and well-developed as its theater offerings, with institutions and venues dedicated to everything from classical symphonies and baroque chamber music to jazz, world music, rock, and electronic beats. The city nurtures both high art and grassroots scenes, ensuring that music lovers always have a rich lineup to explore.

Opéra National du Rhin (ONR)

Headquartered in Strasbourg (with stages in Mulhouse and Colmar), the Opéra National du Rhin is one of France's premier opera companies. Its home stage at the elegant Théâtre Municipal de Strasbourg presents classic operas by Verdi, Mozart, Puccini, and Wagner, as well as lesser-known gems and bold contemporary compositions.

The ONR is internationally recognized for its technical excellence, compelling stagings, and strong ensemble of resident soloists. Opera lovers will appreciate the mix of traditional and daringly modern productions, often accompanied by lavish set design and live orchestration by the *Orchestre Philharmonique de Strasbourg*.

Orchestre Philharmonique de Strasbourg (OPS)

Founded in 1855, this acclaimed orchestra performs a robust annual season of symphonic concerts at the **Palais de la Musique et des Congrès**. Its repertoire spans centuries—from baroque masterworks and Romantic epics to premieres of 21st-century compositions. The OPS also collaborates with visiting soloists and conductors of international repute.

In addition to formal concerts, the orchestra engages in outreach performances, open rehearsals, and family-oriented concerts, making high-quality classical music more accessible to all.

Cité de la Musique et de la Danse

This multipurpose facility is a cornerstone of Strasbourg's musical education and performance scene. Home to the Strasbourg Conservatory, it offers a year-round calendar of recitals, student showcases, ensemble performances, and occasional guest concerts. Visitors can often catch chamber music evenings, jazz ensembles, and contemporary projects in an intimate setting.

Live Music Venues & Nightlife

Beyond the classical stage, Strasbourg is also home to a thriving live music scene that includes jazz clubs, rock bars, and alternative performance spaces. These venues are essential to the city's creative heartbeat and attract both local talent and international acts.

- **Le Molodoï:** A beloved alternative venue that hosts punk, metal, indie, and electronic music events, often organized by local associations. Known for its grassroots ethos and vibrant energy.
- **La Laiterie:** Arguably Strasbourg's most popular contemporary music venue, La Laiterie hosts a wide range of concerts—electronic DJs, rock bands, indie artists, and international touring musicians. Its larger hall accommodates up to 1,000 people, while its Club stage offers more intimate gigs.
- **Jazzdor:** A festival and a label, Jazzdor promotes Strasbourg as a hub for modern jazz. While the main festival happens in November, affiliated concerts and collaborations continue throughout the year at various venues.
- **Blue Note Café and Café Berlin:** These smaller cafés and bars often feature local musicians in genres ranging from acoustic folk to funk, making them great spots for spontaneous musical discoveries.

Seasonal and Outdoor Performances

Strasbourg also embraces performance art beyond the confines of traditional venues. During warmer months, you'll find concerts and theatrical acts in public squares, gardens, and along the banks of the Ill River.

- **Fête de la Musique (June 21):** A nationwide celebration of live music, with dozens of free performances across the city—from solo pianists in courtyards to full orchestras in the squares.
- **Summer Classical Concert Series:** Held in churches and historic buildings like St. Thomas or the Temple Neuf, these concerts offer atmospheric interpretations of sacred and classical works.
- **Open-Air Theater and Street Performances:** Particularly in summer, local theater companies stage productions in the city's parks or plazas—offering an informal and interactive cultural experience.

Tips for Attending Performances in Strasbourg

- **Book Early:** Tickets for high-demand shows at the TNS or the Opéra sell out quickly, particularly on weekends and holidays. It's best to reserve in advance through official websites.
- **Language Considerations:** Theater performances are typically in French, though select productions may include surtitles or language-free physical theater. Musical performances generally transcend language barriers.
- **Dress Code:** Most venues do not enforce a strict dress code, but business casual is standard for evening performances. For operas and opening nights, formal attire is often preferred.

- **Discounts:** Students, seniors, and youth under 26 can often benefit from reduced ticket prices or last-minute student seats.
- **Cultural Passes:** Visitors planning to attend multiple shows might consider local cultural passes or event packages offered by the city's tourism office or cultural venues.

Final Thoughts

Strasbourg's commitment to the performing arts is evident in the depth, range, and quality of its offerings. Whether you're watching a bold contemporary play, settling into a classical concert, or exploring a tucked-away jazz club, the city invites you to participate in its cultural life with open arms. It's not just about attending a show—it's about joining a living, breathing creative tradition that continues to evolve in one of Europe's most artistically vibrant cities.

6.3 Museums & Galleries

Strasbourg is not just a political and historical hub; it is a city deeply rooted in art, heritage, and intellectual tradition. Its museums and galleries reflect the diversity of its cultural legacy—from medieval religious art and Alsatian folk culture to contemporary installations and European political history. Visitors will find institutions that are both internationally significant and intimately local, housed in stunning architecture ranging from baroque palaces to sleek modernist spaces.

Exploring Strasbourg's museums isn't simply about viewing objects; it's about engaging with centuries of thought, creativity, and storytelling. Each venue is curated with a strong sense of place, and together, they present a panoramic view of the city's layered identity.

Musée de l'Œuvre Notre-Dame (Museum of the Work of Notre-Dame)

Located just behind the Strasbourg Cathedral, this museum is devoted to Upper Rhenish fine and decorative arts from the Middle Ages to the Renaissance. Housed in a cluster of historic buildings—some dating to the 14th century—it's one of the oldest museum complexes in France. Visitors will find original statuary from the Cathedral, stained glass panels, altarpieces, religious paintings, and Gothic sculptures. It offers a deep dive into the spiritual and artistic life of the region from 1300 to 1600.

Highlights:

- Original sculptures by Nikolaus Gerhaert and other Gothic masters
- A reconstruction of medieval Strasbourg's artistic workshops
- Restored stained glass from the cathedral's early phases

This museum is essential for those interested in religious art, ecclesiastical architecture, and medieval craftsmanship.

Musée Alsacien (Alsatian Museum)

Set within a series of charming 17th-century townhouses along the Quai Saint-Nicolas, the Musée Alsacien offers an immersive experience into rural Alsatian life. The exhibits cover traditional dress, folk art, farming tools, reconstructed interiors, and seasonal customs from across the region. Particular attention is given to the coexistence of Catholic, Protestant, and Jewish communities.

Key Themes:

- Traditional Alsatian furniture and woodworking

- Wedding customs and seasonal rituals
- Rural life in the Vosges and Rhine Valley

Wandering its creaky staircases and timber-framed rooms feels more like entering someone's home than a formal museum.

Musée d'Art Moderne et Contemporain de Strasbourg (MAMCS)

One of the largest modern art museums in France, MAMCS is a beacon for 19th, 20th, and 21st-century art. Located along the banks of the Ill River, the museum's glass façade and open plan layout create a fluid, inviting atmosphere. The collection includes works by Gustave Doré, Hans Arp, Victor Brauner, and Max Ernst, as well as rotating exhibits of contemporary European and international artists.

What to Expect:

- Impressionist, surrealist, and abstract painting
- Sculpture gardens and a panoramic rooftop terrace
- Multimedia installations and photography exhibits

The museum's café and bookshop are also notable—especially for visitors seeking a quiet moment overlooking the river.

Musée Historique de Strasbourg (Historical Museum of Strasbourg)

Housed in the 16th-century *Ancienne Boucherie*, this museum traces Strasbourg's history from antiquity to the present day. It's exceptionally well-organized and highly interactive, with models, maps, weapons, and artifacts that contextualize the city's development through periods of Roman, Holy Roman Empire, French, and German rule.

Visitor Favorites:

- A giant 18th-century scale model of Strasbourg
- Napoleon's official uniform worn during his 1805 visit
- Themed rooms on printing, military history, and urban planning

It's an excellent starting point for first-time visitors looking to understand Strasbourg's political and cultural complexity.

Palais Rohan Museums (Three Museums in One Site)

The 18th-century *Palais Rohan*, once a prince-bishop's residence, houses three major museums under one roof:

1. **Musée Archéologique** – Located in the basement, this museum covers prehistoric, Roman, and early medieval archaeology of Alsace. It includes tools, ceramics, jewelry, and a remarkable Merovingian collection.
2. **Musée des Beaux-Arts (Fine Arts Museum)** – On the first floor, this museum spans European painting from the 14th to the 19th centuries, with works by Botticelli, El Greco, Rubens, Goya, and Delacroix.
3. **Musée des Arts Décoratifs** – On the ground floor, this museum offers insight into 18th-century aristocratic life through period furnishings, ceramics, timepieces, and decorative objects. Many rooms are preserved in their original décor.

Visitors can purchase a combined ticket or explore each museum separately, depending on interest.

Le Vaisseau (Science Museum for Families & Children)

For those traveling with children, Le Vaisseau is an award-winning interactive science center that transforms learning into play. It covers science, technology, and environment through hundreds of hands-on exhibits. Multilingual explanations (French, German, English) make it accessible to international visitors.

Features:

- Water games and engineering puzzles
- Environmental discovery zones
- Outdoor learning gardens and creative workshops

This is a highly recommended half-day excursion for families.

Galeries and Contemporary Spaces

Beyond institutional museums, Strasbourg is also home to dozens of private galleries, artist-run collectives, and pop-up exhibitions. These spaces frequently feature regional and international artists working in photography, installation, street art, and new media.

- **Galerie Art'Course** – A respected venue for emerging and mid-career contemporary artists.
- **Stimultania** – Specializes in photography exhibitions with a strong focus on social justice themes.
- **Apollonia European Art Exchanges** – Promotes cross-border artistic collaboration between France and Eastern Europe.

Many galleries are concentrated around the Krutenau and Neustadt neighborhoods, making it easy to design a half-day walking tour focused on visual culture.

Practical Information

- **Museum Passes**: The Strasbourg City Pass offers discounted or free admission to many museums. Multi-day regional passes are also available.
- **Opening Days**: Most museums are closed on Tuesdays and public holidays. Always verify schedules before visiting.
- **Language Accessibility**: Major museums offer information panels in French, German, and English. Audioguides are widely available.
- **Discounts**: Students, seniors, and children under 18 typically receive free or reduced admission. Some museums also offer free entry on the first Sunday of each month.

Conclusion

Strasbourg's museums and galleries are not only repositories of knowledge and beauty—they are living spaces where ideas continue to evolve and circulate. Whether you're captivated by medieval iconography, intrigued by modern abstraction, or simply curious about local life, these institutions offer something deeply enriching. Taking the time to explore them will add layers of meaning to your understanding of Strasbourg and the wider Alsace region.

6.4 Guided Tours & River Cruises

Strasbourg is a city that reveals its layers most richly when explored through the lens of a well-curated guided tour or a relaxing river cruise. Whether you're keen on delving into the city's complex Franco-German history, admiring medieval timber-framed architecture, or discovering Strasbourg's role in the modern European Union, there are a wealth of experiences led by locals and experts that can offer a deeper, more meaningful understanding of the region.

Walking Tours: Uncovering Strasbourg by Foot

Walking tours are one of the most immersive ways to explore Strasbourg, particularly within the historic Grande Île and Petite France districts. These guided walks are often led by licensed local guides who are well-versed in Strasbourg's cultural heritage and unique bilingual identity.

- **Historic Center Walking Tour**: Ideal for first-time visitors, this tour typically begins at the Place de la Cathédrale and covers highlights such as the Strasbourg Cathedral, Kammerzell House, Rohan Palace, and the cobbled lanes of Petite France. These tours emphasize Gothic and Renaissance architecture, Strasbourg's UNESCO status, and its religious past.
- **Petite France Guided Walk**: This option focuses solely on one of the most photogenic areas of the city. You'll learn about the tanneries, canals, and

medieval trades that once powered this neighborhood. Many guides also share anecdotes about daily life centuries ago—something you won't find in brochures.

- **European Quarter Tour**: This specialized tour caters to those interested in modern Strasbourg and the European institutions headquartered here. Stops may include the European Parliament, the Council of Europe, and the European Court of Human Rights. Ideal for politically curious travelers and students.

Specialized Themed Tours

For those looking to engage with more niche aspects of Strasbourg, a range of themed guided tours is available:

- **Food & Wine Tours**: Led by culinary guides or sommeliers, these tours often include tastings of Alsatian specialties such as tarte flambée, Munster cheese, and regional wines like Riesling and Gewürztraminer. Tours may include market visits, delicatessen stops, or even vineyard tastings just outside the city.
- **Jewish Heritage Tour**: Strasbourg has a complex Jewish history, dating back to the Middle Ages. This tour sheds light on the Jewish community's contribution to the city, including visits to memorials, historic synagogues, and the Jewish quarter.
- **Ghost Tours & Legends Walks**: For those who enjoy a touch of drama and folklore, some guides offer evening tours that explore Strasbourg's lesser-known ghost stories, urban legends, and strange occurrences.

Bicycle Tours: Strasbourg on Two Wheels

As one of France's most bike-friendly cities, Strasbourg offers an extensive network of cycling paths that make guided bike tours a great option for active travelers.

These tours generally cover more ground than walking tours, reaching outlying areas such as:

- The Neustadt district, showcasing imperial German architecture.
- The Parc de l'Orangerie and surrounding green spaces.
- Scenic routes along the Ill River and around the city's medieval ramparts.

Many of these tours include stops at local cafés or bakeries for a mid-ride refreshment and commentary on urban development and ecological planning in the city.

Boat Tours & River Cruises: Strasbourg from the Water

One of Strasbourg's signature experiences is a river cruise along the Ill River. These leisurely journeys offer visitors a scenic overview of the city while floating past some of its most iconic landmarks.

- **Batorama Cruises**: The most popular river cruise operator in Strasbourg, Batorama offers panoramic boats with both open-air and covered seating, multilingual audio guides, and a loop that takes you through Petite France, the Covered Bridges, the Vauban Dam, the Neustadt, and the European Institutions district.

- **Cruise Features**:
  - Duration: Approximately 70 minutes
  - Commentary available in up to 12 languages
  - Wheelchair accessible boats
  - Family-friendly and stroller-accessible
- **Departure Point**: Place du Marché aux Poissons (near the Cathedral)

Evening cruises, particularly in summer, offer a magical perspective of the city under warm golden light or subtle nighttime illumination. Some boats also offer specialty cruises, such as **Christmas Market river tours** in winter or **private charters** for small groups.

Tips for Booking Guided Tours & Cruises

- **Advance Reservations**: While walk-up availability exists for many boat cruises and public walking tours, it's advisable to book in advance—especially in peak seasons (May–September and December).
- **Language Options**: Ensure the tour is available in your preferred language. Many offer English, French, and German options, but some smaller or more niche tours may only be in French.
- **Combination Packages**: Look for combined tickets that include a walking tour and river cruise, or museum passes bundled with a guided visit. These can offer better value.
- **Local Guide Services**:
  - **Office de Tourisme de Strasbourg**: Offers certified guides and city-approved experiences.
  - **Local tour platforms**: Companies like Viator, GetYourGuide, and local operators often feature authentic, small-group tours with detailed itineraries.

Chapter 7: Where to Stay

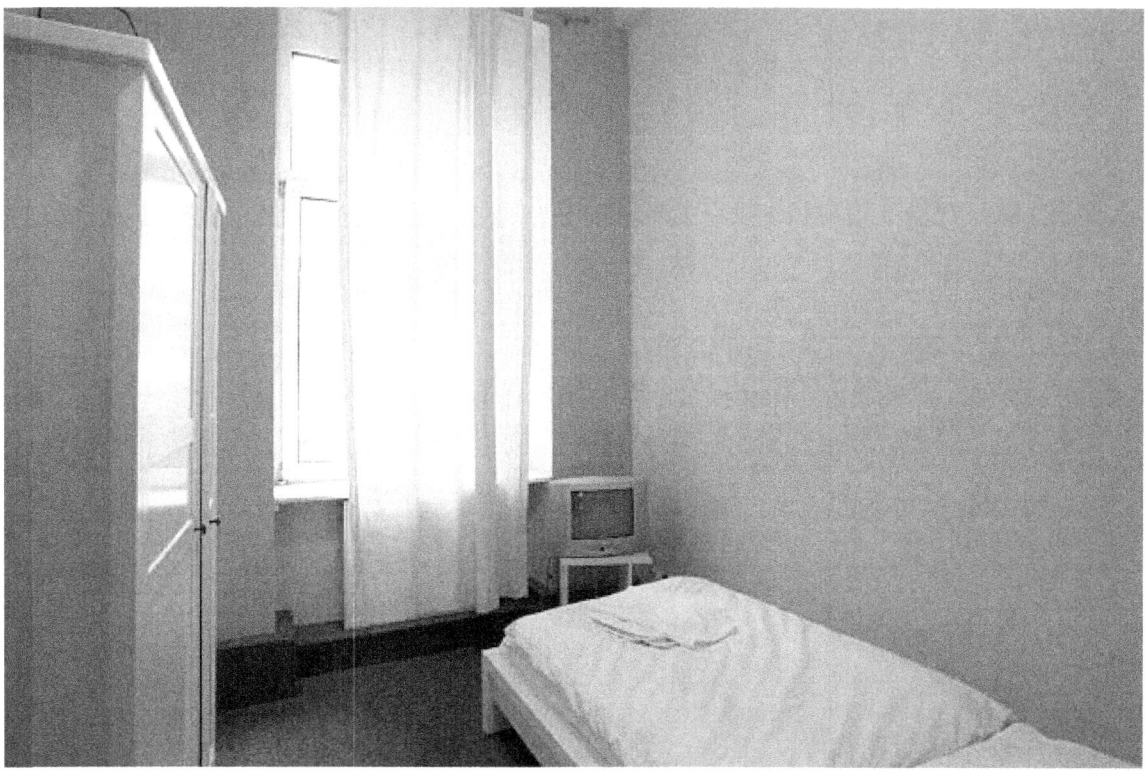

7.1 Best Areas to Stay

Strasbourg offers a wide range of accommodation options that cater to various traveler needs—whether you're after the historical charm of half-timbered houses, proximity to institutions of the European Union, or a quiet escape near green spaces. Choosing the right neighborhood will shape your experience, from riverside views and Gothic cathedrals to buzzing local markets and café terraces. Below are the most prominent and traveler-friendly areas in Strasbourg, along with top-rated places to stay in each.

1. Grande Île – Historic Heart of Strasbourg

Why Stay Here:
Grande Île is Strasbourg's UNESCO-listed city center, a pedestrian-friendly district surrounded by canals. Staying here puts you within walking distance of the Strasbourg Cathedral, the Ill River, Place Kléber, and La Petite France.

Recommended Hotel:
Maison Rouge Strasbourg Hotel & Spa, Autograph Collection

- **Address:** 4 Rue des Francs-Bourgeois, 67000 Strasbourg, France

- **Contact:** +33 3 88 32 08 60
- **Website:** www.maison-rouge.com
- **Price Range:** €180–€300 per night (depending on room type and season)
- **Key Features:** Luxury spa, on-site gourmet restaurant, art deco interiors
- **Visitor Services:** Concierge, luggage storage, business center, valet parking
- **Ideal For:** Couples, business travelers, and first-time visitors

2. La Petite France – Picturesque & Romantic

Why Stay Here:
La Petite France is one of the most photographed quarters in Strasbourg. With its cobbled lanes, timber-framed buildings, and canals, this district offers postcard-worthy scenery with a quiet ambiance, especially in the evening.

Recommended Hotel:
Hôtel & Spa Régent Petite France

- **Address:** 5 Rue des Moulins, 67000 Strasbourg, France
- **Contact:** +33 3 88 76 43 43
- **Website:** www.regent-petite-france.com
- **Price Range:** €200–€350 per night
- **Key Features:** Riverside terrace, full-service spa, panoramic views
- **Visitor Services:** Room service, in-room massage, bicycle rental
- **Ideal For:** Honeymooners, romantic getaways, architecture lovers

3. Neustadt – Imperial Grandeur & Residential Comfort

Why Stay Here:
This area north of Grande Île is known for its wide boulevards, 19th-century buildings, and elegant townhouses. Neustadt is quieter and less touristy, while still offering easy access to the city center and European institutions.

Recommended Hotel:
Hotel D Strasbourg

- **Address:** 15 Rue du Fossé des Treize, 67000 Strasbourg, France
- **Contact:** +33 3 88 24 03 40
- **Website:** www.hotel-d.com
- **Price Range:** €140–€220 per night
- **Key Features:** Modern design, wellness area, eco-conscious amenities
- **Visitor Services:** Fitness room, parking, pet-friendly options
- **Ideal For:** Professionals, solo travelers, longer stays

4. European Quarter – Diplomacy & Green Spaces

Why Stay Here:
This modern district is home to the European Parliament, the Council of Europe, and Parc de l'Orangerie. It's ideal for business travelers or those wanting a more peaceful environment with plenty of greenery.

Recommended Hotel:
Hôtel de l'Orangerie

- **Address:** 58 Allée de la Robertsau, 67000 Strasbourg, France
- **Contact:** +33 3 88 35 20 20
- **Website:** www.hotelorangerie.com
- **Price Range:** €100–€160 per night
- **Key Features:** Residential charm, close to park, personalized service
- **Visitor Services:** Free parking, laundry service, airport shuttle
- **Ideal For:** Diplomats, park lovers, families

5. Krutenau – Bohemian & Student-Friendly

Why Stay Here:
Krutenau is a lively neighborhood with a youthful energy, thanks to its universities, art schools, and creative spaces. It's perfect for those looking for nightlife, independent shops, and a more local vibe.

Recommended Hotel:
Hôtel Diana Dauphine

- **Address:** 30 Rue de la 1ère Armée, 67000 Strasbourg, France
- **Contact:** +33 3 88 36 26 61
- **Website:** www.hotel-diana-dauphine.com
- **Price Range:** €110–€180 per night
- **Key Features:** Trendy decor, city views, breakfast buffet
- **Visitor Services:** Secure parking, multilingual staff, early check-in
- **Ideal For:** Young travelers, creatives, weekend explorers

6. Gare Centrale – Convenient & Well-Connected

Why Stay Here:

Located around the main train station (Gare de Strasbourg), this area is practical for travelers arriving by rail or needing quick access to public transport. While less scenic, it's safe, efficient, and affordable.

Recommended Hotel:
Le Grand Hôtel

- **Address:** 12 Place de la Gare, 67000 Strasbourg, France
- **Contact:** +33 3 88 52 84 84
- **Website:** www.legrandhotel.fr
- **Price Range:** €90–€150 per night
- **Key Features:** Central location, modern rooms, good breakfast
- **Visitor Services:** 24-hour reception, business services, nearby restaurants
- **Ideal For:** Short stays, business trips, travelers on a moderate budget

7. Robertsau – Quiet & Residential

Why Stay Here:

Robertsau is a calm, green suburb north of the European Quarter. It's ideal for those looking for a peaceful atmosphere while still being within reach of the city center via tram or car.

Recommended Hotel:
Le Jean-Sébastien Bach Residence

- **Address:** 6 Boulevard Jean-Sébastien Bach, 67000 Strasbourg, France
- **Contact:** +33 3 88 45 35 88
- **Website:** www.residencebach.com
- **Price Range:** €95–€160 per night
- **Key Features:** Apartment-style rooms, kitchenette, extended stays
- **Visitor Services:** Daily housekeeping, secure parking, laundry facilities
- **Ideal For:** Families, long-term travelers, remote workers

Final Thoughts

Choosing where to stay in Strasbourg depends on your travel priorities—whether that's cultural immersion, business access, or scenic tranquility. Grande Île and La Petite France place you at the city's heart, while Neustadt and Robertsau offer calm and elegance. Krutenau is vibrant and artsy, whereas the European Quarter delivers peace and proximity to major institutions.

Each area has its unique appeal, and the city's excellent public transport ensures that no matter where you stay, you're never far from the action.

7.2 Hotels (Luxury, Mid-Range, Budget)

Strasbourg's hospitality scene is rich and varied. Whether you're seeking five-star luxury with indulgent spa treatments and Michelin-starred dining, a charming mid-range boutique hotel close to landmarks, or a clean, budget-friendly room that doesn't skimp on convenience, the city offers dependable options at every level. Below is a curated list of top-rated hotels in each category—designed to match a wide range of travel styles.

Luxury Hotels (€200 and up per night)

1. Hôtel Régent Petite France & Spa

- **Address:** 5 Rue des Moulins, 67000 Strasbourg, France
- **Contact:** +33 3 88 76 43 43
- **Website:** www.regent-petite-france.com
- **Average Price:** €240–€370 per night
- **Key Features:** 5-star comfort, riverside views, full-service spa, elegant décor
- **Visitor Services:** Valet parking, concierge, massage therapy, gourmet dining

- **Ideal For:** Couples, special occasions, high-end travelers

2. Sofitel Strasbourg Grande Île

- **Address:** 4 Place Saint-Pierre-le-Jeune, 67000 Strasbourg, France
- **Contact:** +33 3 88 15 49 00
- **Website:** www.sofitel-strasbourg.com
- **Average Price:** €220–€350 per night
- **Key Features:** Central location, luxury linens, rooftop terrace, fitness center
- **Visitor Services:** 24-hour room service, airport transfers, multilingual staff
- **Ideal For:** Business travelers, luxury seekers, families

3. Pavillon Régent Petite France

- **Address:** 6 Rue des Moulins, 67000 Strasbourg, France
- **Contact:** +33 3 88 76 43 43
- **Website:** www.pavillon-regent.com
- **Average Price:** €210–€280 per night
- **Key Features:** Boutique charm, riverside balconies, personalized service
- **Visitor Services:** Breakfast in-room, luggage assistance, bicycle rentals
- **Ideal For:** Design-conscious travelers, relaxed stays

Mid-Range Hotels (€100–€180 per night)

1. Hotel Gutenberg

- **Address:** 31 Rue des Serruriers, 67000 Strasbourg, France
- **Contact:** +33 3 88 32 17 15
- **Website:** www.hotel-gutenberg.com
- **Average Price:** €120–€160 per night
- **Key Features:** Next to the cathedral, modern rooms, family-friendly
- **Visitor Services:** Free Wi-Fi, luggage storage, business center
- **Ideal For:** Sightseers, families, weekend travelers

2. BOMA easy living hotel

- **Address:** 7 Rue du 22 Novembre, 67000 Strasbourg, France
- **Contact:** +33 3 90 00 10 00
- **Website:** www.boma-hotel.com

- **Average Price:** €130–€170 per night
- **Key Features:** Urban and colorful décor, eco-friendly philosophy, casual dining
- **Visitor Services:** Self-check-in, on-site fitness room, coworking lounge
- **Ideal For:** Young travelers, digital nomads, creative professionals

3. Hotel D Strasbourg

- **Address:** 15 Rue du Fossé des Treize, 67000 Strasbourg, France
- **Contact:** +33 3 88 24 03 40
- **Website:** www.hotel-d.com
- **Average Price:** €140–€180 per night
- **Key Features:** Sleek interior, wellness area, eco-conscious services
- **Visitor Services:** Sauna, private parking, express check-in
- **Ideal For:** Professionals, solo travelers, longer stays

Budget Hotels (Under €100 per night)

1. ibis Strasbourg Centre Historique

- **Address:** 7 Rue de Molsheim, 67000 Strasbourg, France
- **Contact:** +33 3 90 22 48 70
- **Website:** www.ibis.com
- **Average Price:** €65–€95 per night
- **Key Features:** Basic comfort, close to Petite France, 24-hour reception
- **Visitor Services:** Budget-friendly breakfast, accessible rooms, pet-friendly
- **Ideal For:** Budget-conscious travelers, quick stopovers

2. Hotel Suisse Strasbourg

- **Address:** 2-4 Rue de la Râpe, 67000 Strasbourg, France
- **Contact:** +33 3 88 35 22 11
- **Website:** www.hotel-suisse.com
- **Average Price:** €85–€100 per night
- **Key Features:** Quaint and cozy atmosphere, historic building
- **Visitor Services:** Breakfast room, personalized staff service, terrace seating
- **Ideal For:** Solo explorers, budget-minded culture lovers

3. Hotel Victoria

- **Address:** 7 Rue du Maire Kuss, 67000 Strasbourg, France
- **Contact:** +33 3 88 32 13 06
- **Website:** www.hotel-victoria-strasbourg.com
- **Average Price:** €70–€90 per night
- **Key Features:** Near train station, comfortable rooms, local cafés nearby
- **Visitor Services:** Luggage storage, early check-in, multilingual staff
- **Ideal For:** Backpackers, train travelers, short city breaks

Final Notes on Booking

- **Booking Tips:** Book well in advance during major events such as the Christmas Market (late November to December) and European Parliament sessions.
- **Cancellation Policies:** Always check individual hotel cancellation rules, especially for non-refundable rates.
- **City Tax:** Note that most Strasbourg hotels charge a small daily tourist tax (€1.65–€3 per person, per night).

7.3 Boutique Hotels & Guesthouses

Strasbourg offers a generous selection of boutique hotels and guesthouses, perfect for travelers who value style, intimacy, and character over size or chain branding. Many of these accommodations are family-run or independently managed, offering personalized service and a more authentic sense of place. Whether situated in a centuries-old timber-framed building or a newly restored residence, these properties often reflect the unique architectural and cultural richness of the Alsace region.

Below is a selection of some of Strasbourg's most distinctive and highly rated boutique hotels and guesthouses, suitable for couples, solo travelers, and small families seeking a quiet, comfortable, and curated stay.

1. Hotel Cour du Corbeau – MGallery

- **Address:** 6-8 Rue des Couples, 67000 Strasbourg, France
- **Contact:** +33 3 90 00 26 26
- **Website:** www.cour-corbeau.com
- **Price Range:** €180–€280 per night

Key Features:

This 16th-century former coaching inn has been exquisitely restored into one of Strasbourg's most prestigious boutique hotels. Located just steps from the cathedral and the river, it blends historic Alsatian charm with modern refinement.

Visitor Services:

Concierge, room service, private parking, breakfast served in a vaulted cellar, family suites, free Wi-Fi, pet-friendly accommodations.

Ideal For: Travelers looking for a romantic, historical setting with elegant interiors and five-star attention to detail.

2. Hotel Rohan

- **Address:** 17–19 Rue du Maroquin, 67000 Strasbourg, France
- **Contact:** +33 3 88 32 85 11
- **Website:** www.hotel-rohan.com
- **Price Range:** €130–€180 per night

Key Features:

A boutique gem just a minute's walk from Strasbourg Cathedral, Hotel Rohan offers stylish rooms with refined furnishings, artistic flair, and subtle nods to Alsatian heritage.

Visitor Services:

On-site café with patio dining, multilingual staff, secure luggage storage, 24-hour reception, business corner, pet-friendly options.

Ideal For: Culture lovers, art enthusiasts, and visitors who want to stay in the historic heart of Strasbourg.

3. Hôtel Suisse Strasbourg

- **Address:** 2-4 Rue de la Râpe, 67000 Strasbourg, France
- **Contact:** +33 3 88 35 22 11
- **Website:** www.hotel-suisse.com
- **Price Range:** €90–€120 per night

Key Features:

A charming family-run hotel located near the Cathedral, Hôtel Suisse feels more like a guesthouse, with a warm ambiance and individually decorated rooms. The half-timbered exterior and small courtyard café offer a sense of traditional Alsace.

Visitor Services:
Homemade breakfast, terrace seating, laundry services, bike storage, personalized recommendations from staff, free Wi-Fi.

Ideal For: Solo travelers, mature couples, and visitors who enjoy quiet character-filled properties.

4. Le Bouclier d'Or Boutique Hotel & Spa

- **Address:** 1 Rue du Bouclier, 67000 Strasbourg, France
- **Contact:** +33 3 88 13 73 55
- **Website:** www.hotelboucierdor.com
- **Price Range:** €170–€230 per night

Key Features:
Located in the picturesque La Petite France district, this boutique hotel features antique furnishings, soundproofed rooms, and a full-service spa. It successfully marries 18th-century style with modern comfort.

Visitor Services:
Wellness area with sauna, jacuzzi, and massage services; lounge bar with regional wines; gourmet breakfast; elevator; accessible rooms.

Ideal For: Luxury travelers looking for an elegant retreat in a quiet and romantic setting.

5. Hôtel Beaucour

- **Address:** 5 Rue des Bouchers, 67000 Strasbourg, France
- **Contact:** +33 3 88 76 72 00
- **Website:** www.hotel-beaucour.com
- **Price Range:** €110–€160 per night

Key Features:
Set in a charming Alsatian-style building with a flower-filled courtyard, Hôtel Beaucour is known for its colorful and individually designed rooms—some with spa tubs and four-poster beds.

Visitor Services:
Jacuzzi suites, buffet breakfast, pet-friendly rooms, nearby public parking, business meeting facilities, complimentary Wi-Fi.

Ideal For: Romantic getaways, small business groups, creative travelers looking for a colorful escape.

6. Les Haras Hotel

- **Address:** 23 Rue des Glacières, 67000 Strasbourg, France
- **Contact:** +33 3 90 20 50 00
- **Website:** www.les-haras-hotel.com
- **Price Range:** €160–€220 per night

Key Features:

Set in a former royal stud farm, this design-led boutique hotel offers a blend of equestrian heritage and modern architectural flair. Rooms feature natural materials, clean lines, and a warm, earthy color palette.

Visitor Services:

On-site brasserie, spa access, wellness treatments, valet parking, breakfast buffet, multilingual front desk.

Ideal For: Design-savvy visitors, architecture lovers, and couples looking for a serene, upscale escape.

Choosing a Boutique Stay in Strasbourg

Boutique hotels and guesthouses in Strasbourg often book out quickly—particularly during the city's high seasons (May to September and December). It's advisable to book early, especially for historic or well-reviewed properties. These establishments offer excellent alternatives to mainstream hotels, with the benefit of distinct personality and tailored guest experiences.

7.4 Short-Term Rentals & Hostels

Strasbourg offers a diverse range of accommodations that cater to independent travelers, backpackers, digital nomads, and families seeking more flexible or budget-conscious lodging options. Short-term rentals and hostels continue to be popular choices, particularly for visitors planning extended stays, group travel, or those prioritizing community and affordability without compromising comfort or location.

Both short-term apartments and hostels in Strasbourg benefit from the city's walkability, with many properties located within or near the historic center, the university quarter, and the bustling Krutenau and Petite France districts.

Short-Term Rentals in Strasbourg

Short-term rentals are ideal for travelers looking for autonomy, space, and a home-like setting. These include furnished apartments, studio flats, lofts, and entire homes—many available through platforms like Airbnb, Vrbo, and Booking.com.

Benefits of Short-Term Rentals:

- **Self-Catering Facilities:** Most units come with fully equipped kitchens or kitchenettes, perfect for travelers who prefer cooking or staying for multiple days.

- **Cost-Effective for Groups or Families:** Multiple beds and private common spaces reduce the need to book multiple hotel rooms.
- **Local Immersion:** Rentals in residential neighborhoods allow visitors to experience Strasbourg like a local, often near markets, bakeries, and tram stops.

Popular Areas for Rentals:

- **La Petite France:** Offers picturesque views and historic charm.
- **Krutenau:** Popular with students and younger travelers; lively yet less touristy.
- **Neudorf & Orangerie:** Quieter, more residential areas that are well-connected by tram.

Approximate Price Range:

- **Studios & 1-bed apartments:** €70–€130 per night
- **2–3 bedroom apartments or lofts:** €120–€250 per night
- **Luxury or historic properties:** €200+ per night

Tips for Booking:

- Book early, especially during major festivals or December's Christmas market.
- Confirm whether local taxes (taxe de séjour) are included in the nightly rate.
- Look for listings with strong guest reviews, clear cancellation policies, and well-documented amenities.

Hostels in Strasbourg

Hostels are a smart and social choice for solo travelers, students, or anyone traveling on a modest budget. Strasbourg's hostels are generally clean, well-managed, and centrally located, offering private and dorm-style accommodations with communal kitchens, lounges, and organized events or walking tours.

Here are some reputable hostels worth considering:

1. The People – Strasbourg

- **Address:** 7 Rue de la Krutenau, 67000 Strasbourg, France
- **Contact:** +33 3 88 88 52 30
- **Website:** www.thepeoplehostel.com
- **Price Range:** €25–€40 per night (dorms), €80–€120 (private rooms)

Key Features:

Located in a former tobacco factory, this vibrant hostel blends industrial design with comfort. It features a café-bar, shared kitchen, co-working space, and live music events. The riverfront location near the university and Old Town is ideal for young and social travelers.

Visitor Services:

Free Wi-Fi, lockers, luggage storage, linen provided, bike rental, wheelchair-accessible common areas.

2. Ciarus

- **Address:** 7 Rue Finkmatt, 67000 Strasbourg, France
- **Contact:** +33 3 88 21 61 02
- **Website:** www.ciarus.com
- **Price Range:** €30–€45 per night (shared dorms), €80–€110 (private rooms)

Key Features:

Ciarus is a clean and modern hostel with hotel-style infrastructure. Ideal for school groups, solo travelers, or international guests, it has a multilingual staff, in-house restaurant, and 24/7 reception. It's within a 10-minute walk of the cathedral.

Visitor Services:

Daily housekeeping, secure card access, elevator, conference rooms, breakfast buffet available, free Wi-Fi throughout.

3. Résidence de l'Université (Budget Dorm Option)

- **Address:** Rue de l'Université, 67000 Strasbourg, France
- **Contact:** Typically seasonal, booking via university-affiliated programs or youth travel sites
- **Price Range:** €20–€35 per night (dormitory-style rooms)

Key Features:

This student residence occasionally opens its rooms during summer breaks or low seasons for travelers. Basic but safe, it offers excellent access to both the university and the historic core.

Visitor Services:

Shared bathrooms and kitchens, security monitoring, basic linens, Wi-Fi (may require setup).

Choosing Between Rentals and Hostels

Criteria	Short-Term Rentals	Hostels
Best For	Families, couples, long stays	Solo travelers, students
Privacy Level	High	Low to medium
Facilities	Full kitchen, private bath	Shared bath, social lounge
Cost Efficiency	Better for groups	Better for single-night stays
Social Interaction	Minimal	High (communal setting)

Final Thoughts

Whether you're seeking the flexibility of an apartment, the community feel of a hostel, or a combination of both, Strasbourg delivers a range of smart and accessible options. Be mindful of seasonal availability, as accommodations tend to book out quickly during large events like the **Christmas Market** or **European Parliament sessions**. For travelers who value convenience and local atmosphere, both short-term rentals and hostels offer a practical and rewarding base from which to explore the city.

Chapter 8: Food & Drink in Strasbourg

8.1 Traditional Alsatian Cuisine

Strasbourg's culinary identity is as rich and multifaceted as its cultural heritage. Positioned at the crossroads of France and Germany, the city's gastronomy reflects a harmonious blend of French refinement and hearty German traditions. Alsatian cuisine is renowned for its generous portions, robust flavors, and emphasis on local ingredients—often served in charming winstubs (rustic taverns) where the atmosphere is as much a part of the experience as the food.

Whether you're savoring a crisp tarte flambée in a centuries-old eatery or sipping a glass of local Riesling with a plate of choucroute garnie, dining in Strasbourg offers more than just a meal—it's a deep dive into the region's story.

A Blend of Two Worlds

Alsatian cuisine is heavily influenced by the region's history, particularly its oscillating ties between France and Germany. This has led to a unique food culture that combines

Germanic heartiness (think sausages, potatoes, and sauerkraut) with French culinary techniques and presentation.

Local dishes are typically built around seasonal and regional ingredients: cabbage, pork, duck, onions, mushrooms, dairy, and freshwater fish from the Rhine and Ill rivers. Butter and cream are generously used, and you'll often find slow-cooked or braised preparations that highlight time-honored methods.

Iconic Alsatian Dishes to Try

Choucroute Garnie (Sauerkraut with Meats)

Perhaps the most iconic Alsatian dish, this plate features a mountain of fermented cabbage stewed in white wine and spices, topped with an assortment of cured meats and sausages—smoked pork shoulder, knack sausages, frankfurters, and sometimes even goose or ham hocks. It's both a comfort food and a cultural staple.

Tarte Flambée (Flammekueche)

This Alsatian flatbread is often compared to pizza, but it's far more delicate and rooted in rural tradition. A thin crust is topped with crème fraîche, onions, and lardons (bacon strips), then baked in a wood-fired oven until golden and bubbling. Variations may include mushrooms, Munster cheese, or even sweet renditions with apples and cinnamon.

Baeckeoffe

This slow-cooked casserole is made from a hearty mix of marinated pork, lamb, and beef with potatoes, onions, and leeks, all simmered in white wine and sealed in a terrine. Traditionally, it was prepared on Sundays or holidays and left to bake in the baker's oven—hence the name, which translates to "baker's oven."

Coq au Riesling

A regional twist on the classic French dish coq au vin, this version swaps red wine for the region's signature white Riesling. The chicken is stewed with mushrooms, cream, and shallots, resulting in a light yet rich dish that pairs beautifully with local wines.

Munster Cheese

Strong-smelling and soft-textured, Munster is a bold cow's milk cheese made in the Vosges mountains. It's often served with caraway seeds or melted over potatoes in hot dishes. While its aroma is potent, its flavor is surprisingly smooth and earthy.

Spaetzle

A nod to German cuisine, these soft egg noodles or dumplings are typically served as a side dish with meat stews or in buttery sauces. They are a comforting staple in many Alsatian homes.

Regional Sweets & Desserts

Kougelhopf

This tall, crown-shaped brioche-like cake is a regional favorite. Often baked in a fluted ceramic mold, it's filled with raisins, almonds, and sometimes a splash of kirsch (cherry liqueur). Lightly sweet, it's often eaten for breakfast or with coffee in the afternoon.

Bretzel

Not just a snack, but a cultural icon—Alsatian pretzels are crisp on the outside, soft inside, and often served with mustard, cheese, or even sliced meats. Look for them at markets and street vendors.

Pain d'épices

A spiced gingerbread loaf made with honey and a mix of cinnamon, cloves, and anise. Popular during the Christmas season but available year-round, it's often eaten plain or with a smear of butter.

Tarte aux Myrtilles (Blueberry Tart)

A seasonal favorite from the Vosges region, this tart features fresh mountain blueberries atop a buttery crust, sometimes finished with a light cream topping or dusted with powdered sugar.

Accompanying Drinks

Alsace Wines

Strasbourg sits at the northern edge of the Alsace Wine Route, and wine is central to its food culture. Crisp, aromatic whites are the region's specialty:

- **Riesling:** Dry, mineral-driven, and perfect with sauerkraut or fish.
- **Gewürztraminer:** Floral and spicy, pairs well with Munster cheese or foie gras.
- **Pinot Gris & Muscat:** Full-bodied wines with orchard-fruit flavors.

- **Crémant d'Alsace:** A sparkling wine made in the traditional Champagne method, often served as an apéritif.

Beer

The region is also known for its brewing traditions. Strasbourg is home to several well-known breweries, including Kronenbourg. You'll find a variety of pilsners, wheat beers, and seasonal brews in local taverns and beer gardens.

Eaux-de-Vie

These clear fruit brandies—made from cherries, plums, or pears—are commonly offered as a digestif after a heavy Alsatian meal.

Dining Traditions & Etiquette

- **Winstubs** are traditional Alsatian eateries with cozy wooden interiors and handwritten menus. Reservations are recommended, especially in popular areas like Petite France.
- **Lunch** is usually served between 12:00 PM and 2:00 PM; **dinner** typically starts from 7:00 PM.
- It's customary to say "Bonjour" when entering a shop or restaurant, and "Merci, au revoir" when leaving.
- Tipping is not obligatory, but rounding up or leaving 5–10% for good service is appreciated.

Conclusion

Dining in Strasbourg is not just about food—it's an entry point to the region's soul. From the time-honored dishes served in family-run winstubs to the elegant interpretations found in Michelin-starred restaurants, the city's culinary scene captures the heart of Alsace. Whether you're indulging in creamy sauces or sipping white wine at a terrace café, you'll find that each bite tells a story of tradition, territory, and timeless hospitality.

8.2 Top Restaurants & Cafés in Strasbourg

Strasbourg's culinary landscape reflects its rich Franco-German heritage and cosmopolitan spirit. The city boasts a vibrant array of eateries—ranging from traditional Alsatian winstubs and Michelin-starred establishments to stylish cafés and contemporary bistros. Whether you're seeking refined tasting menus, comfort food with a local twist, or a quiet spot to sip espresso, Strasbourg caters to every palate and preference.

Below is a curated selection of top restaurants and cafés in Strasbourg, recognized for their quality, atmosphere, service, and dedication to regional and seasonal ingredients.

Fine Dining & Gastronomic Restaurants

Au Crocodile

- **Location**: 10 Rue de l'Outre, 67000 Strasbourg
- **Price Range**: €€€€
- **Website**: www.au-crocodile.com
- **Reservation Recommended**: Yes

This Michelin-starred institution is one of Strasbourg's culinary crown jewels. The elegant interior, marked by crisp linens and polished service, sets the stage for a refined dining experience. Expect seasonal tasting menus that highlight Alsatian flavors through a modern French lens. Signature dishes often include truffle-infused game, fresh-caught river fish, and meticulously plated desserts.

Le Gavroche

- **Location**: 4 Rue Klein, 67000 Strasbourg
- **Price Range**: €€€
- **Website**: www.restaurantgavroche.com

Located near the Place Broglie, Le Gavroche offers a gourmet experience in an intimate and contemporary setting. The chef combines traditional Alsatian recipes with modern flair, often using fresh herbs, wild mushrooms, and locally sourced proteins. It's a favorite among locals for celebratory dinners and romantic evenings.

Authentic Alsatian Winstubs

Winstub S'Kaechele

- **Location**: 8 Rue de l'Argile, 67000 Strasbourg
- **Price Range**: €€
- **Website**: skaechele.fr

This family-run winstub is a hidden gem tucked into a quiet alley near the historic center. The ambiance is cozy and rustic, with timber walls and checkered tablecloths. Dishes like duck confit, tarte flambée, and choucroute garnie are prepared according to age-old recipes. The wine list features a thoughtful selection of Alsatian whites.

Maison Kammerzell

- **Location**: 16 Place de la Cathédrale, 67000 Strasbourg
- **Price Range**: €€–€€€
- **Website**: www.maison-kammerzell.com

Housed in a 15th-century timber-framed building just beside the cathedral, Maison Kammerzell offers traditional cuisine in one of Strasbourg's most iconic locations. Their house specialty—Choucroute aux Trois Poissons (sauerkraut with three types of fish)—is renowned. The interior, rich in wood carvings and stained glass, offers a memorable backdrop for visitors.

Modern Bistros & Trendy Eateries

Pur Etc.

- **Location**: 6 Place St. Étienne, 67000 Strasbourg
- **Price Range**: €–€€
- **Website**: www.pur-etc.fr

A modern, eco-conscious eatery focused on farm-to-table principles, Pur Etc. serves a rotating menu of soups, quiches, salads, and stews made with regional organic ingredients. It's popular with students, freelancers, and health-conscious diners. Vegetarian and vegan options are always available.

La Corde à Linge

- **Location**: 2 Place Benjamin Zix, 67000 Strasbourg (La Petite France)
- **Price Range**: €€
- **Website**: www.lacordealinge.com

Located along the scenic canals of Petite France, this restaurant is known for its inviting terrace and Alsatian comfort food with a twist. Their spaetzle variations (especially with Munster cheese or creamy mushroom sauce) are highly recommended. It's casual, lively, and ideal for a long lunch or relaxed dinner.

Charming Cafés & Coffee Shops

Café Bretelles

- **Location**: 36 Rue du Bain aux Plantes, 67000 Strasbourg
- **Price Range**: €
- **Website**: www.cafebretelles.fr

A small but beloved coffee shop nestled in La Petite France, Café Bretelles offers expertly brewed espresso, creative lattes, and homemade pastries in a warm, hipster-friendly setting. It's the kind of place where locals come to read or work, and baristas are passionate about their beans.

Oh My Goodness!

- **Location**: 27 Rue des Juifs, 67000 Strasbourg
- **Price Range**: €
- **Instagram**: @ohmygoodnesscoffee

A stylish café and brunch spot with a minimalist Nordic décor. They serve freshly baked pastries, avocado toast, granola bowls, and strong coffee. Ideal for breakfast meetings or a midday break, it's also popular with tourists seeking a lighter, health-forward option.

Boulangerie Woerlé

- **Location**: 21 Rue des Frères, 67000 Strasbourg
- **Price Range**: €

Though technically a bakery, Woerlé is a local favorite for coffee and viennoiseries. Their kougelhopf and tarte aux myrtilles are crowd-pleasers, and their outdoor bench seating allows for quiet street-side indulgence.

Evening Drinks & Wine Bars

Le Tire-Bouchon

- **Location**: 5 Rue des Tailleurs de Pierre, 67000 Strasbourg
- **Price Range**: €€
- **Website**: www.letirebouchon.fr

A classic winstub offering a robust wine list and hearty Alsatian fare, it transforms into a wine-centric venue in the evening. The ambiance is welcoming, with traditional wood-paneled interiors and attentive staff. Local wines can be ordered by the glass or bottle, and staff are happy to offer pairing suggestions.

Code Bar

- **Location**: 1A Rue Munch, 67000 Strasbourg
- **Price Range**: €€
- **Website**: www.codebar.fr

For craft cocktails and contemporary flair, Code Bar is among the top spots in Strasbourg's nightlife scene. Located just off the river, it's known for its inventive drinks, low lighting, and international clientele. A great way to close out a day of sightseeing.

Conclusion

Strasbourg's restaurant and café scene is a reflection of the city itself—diverse, historical, and full of character. Whether you're sitting beneath exposed timber beams sipping Riesling, or enjoying a latte in a sleek café, every dining moment in Strasbourg tells a story. For travelers looking to explore beyond the attractions, delving into the city's food culture is essential—and often unforgettable.

8.3 Local Wines & Breweries

Strasbourg, located in the heart of the Alsace region, is perfectly positioned along the celebrated *Route des Vins d'Alsace* (Alsace Wine Route), making it one of the most wine-forward cities in France. The area is internationally known for its crisp white wines, centuries-old winegrowing traditions, and charming, family-run wineries. But in addition to its wine heritage, Strasbourg also boasts a growing craft beer scene, honoring both French and German brewing influences.

This section explores the unique wine and beer culture in Strasbourg, offering insights into must-try varietals, prominent local wineries, urban breweries, and where to enjoy a glass—whether you're a casual taster or a devoted connoisseur.

Alsace Wine: A Regional Staple

The Alsace region is best known for its white wines, made predominantly from aromatic grape varieties. The following are among the most recognized:

- **Riesling**: Dry, mineral-driven, and citrusy. Ideal with local dishes like choucroute or river fish.

- **Gewürztraminer**: Spicy, floral, and full-bodied with lychee and rose notes. Pairs beautifully with strong cheeses like Munster.
- **Pinot Gris**: Rich, smoky, and well-structured. Excellent with poultry or foie gras.
- **Sylvaner**: Light and refreshing. Often enjoyed with cold cuts or salads.
- **Crémant d'Alsace**: A sparkling white wine made using the traditional méthode champenoise. A common aperitif in Strasbourg restaurants.

These wines are generally bottled in tall, slender "flûte d'Alsace" bottles, and nearly all are labeled by grape variety, making it easier for visitors to navigate the selection.

Where to Sample Alsace Wines in Strasbourg

Le DiVin

- **Location**: 15 Rue des Tonneliers, 67000 Strasbourg
- **Description**: An intimate and elegantly styled wine bar with a focus on Alsace wines, offering curated flights, pairing plates, and sommelier-led tastings.
- **Specialty**: Small-batch producers and rare vintages.

Cave Historique des Hospices de Strasbourg

- **Location**: 1 Place de l'Hôpital, 67000 Strasbourg
- **Hours**: Mon–Fri, 8:30 AM–12 PM, 1:30 PM–5:30 PM
- **Website**: www.vins-des-hospices-de-strasbourg.fr
- **Highlights**: Located in a 14th-century wine cellar beneath the city hospital, this unique site serves both as a historical attraction and a working winery. Their wines, once made to help fund hospital care, are still sold and enjoyed today. They even house one of the world's oldest aging wines (dating back to 1472).

Vino Strada

- **Location**: 1 Rue des Dentelles, 67000 Strasbourg
- **Vibe**: A relaxed, unpretentious wine bar and café, popular among locals for post-work glasses and platters of regional charcuterie.

Recommended Local Wineries Near Strasbourg

While Strasbourg itself isn't a wine-producing town, many vineyards lie within an hour's drive:

- **Domaine Zind-Humbrecht** (Turckheim): One of Alsace's most respected biodynamic estates, known for bold, expressive whites.

- **Domaine Weinbach** (Kaysersberg): Family-owned, with a focus on terroir and tradition. Their Rieslings and Gewürztraminers are frequently award-winning.
- **Domaine Albert Boxler** (Niedermorschwihr): A boutique producer whose handcrafted wines have a loyal international following.

Strasbourg's Beer Scene

Although wine reigns supreme, Strasbourg has a robust brewing tradition rooted in centuries of German influence. The city was once home to the renowned *Kronenbourg* brewery and has embraced a craft beer revival in recent years, with several microbreweries and taprooms dotting the city.

Brasserie Perle

- **Location**: 21 Rue de l'Industrie, 68310 Holtzheim (just outside Strasbourg)
- **Website**: www.brasserie-perle.com
- **Profile**: A family-run craft brewery founded in 1882 and revived in the 21st century. Perle produces a range of bold, innovative beers—from classic lagers to IPA-style creations—with local ingredients and sustainable methods.

Bendorf Brasserie Artisanale

- **Location**: 115 Rue Jean-Jaurès, 67100 Strasbourg
- **Style**: Experimental, artisanal brewing with Belgian and French styles. Their beers are unfiltered, unpasteurized, and often produced in limited editions.
- **Popular Picks**: Pale ales, porters, and creative seasonal releases.

Les Intenables

- **Location**: Available in many local bars and shops; brewed nearby in Ostwald
- **About**: This collective of craft brewers focuses on nonconformist, intensely flavored beers, offering options that include imperial stouts, double IPAs, and sour ales.

Craft Beer & Wine Bars Worth Visiting

- **Académie de la Bière**: A beloved bar with dozens of taps and hundreds of bottled options. Perfect for beer enthusiasts looking to try local and international selections side by side.
- **Beer O'Clock Strasbourg**: A self-pour beer bar near the cathedral where visitors use prepaid cards to sample from rotating taps.
- **La Lanterne**: One of the oldest beer-focused spots in town with a rustic ambiance and Alsatian charm.

Conclusion

Whether you're sampling a crisp Riesling in a centuries-old cellar, sipping on Gewürztraminer with a slice of tarte flambée, or trying a craft saison brewed just a few streets away, Strasbourg offers an exceptional experience for lovers of both wine and beer. The city encourages tasting, conversation, and discovery—making every sip part of the broader story of Alsatian culture.

8.4 Markets & Street Food

Strasbourg's culinary charm doesn't reside solely in fine dining restaurants or cozy winstubs—it also thrives in its vibrant open-air markets, food halls, and emerging street food culture. These spaces are where tradition meets spontaneity, where locals shop for fresh produce, regional cheeses, and artisanal breads, and where visitors can sample authentic Alsatian fare on the go.

From seasonal Christmas markets brimming with hearty specialties to year-round farmers' markets alive with color and aroma, Strasbourg's market and street food scenes offer a flavorful window into daily life in the Alsace capital.

Traditional Markets in Strasbourg

Strasbourg's markets are as diverse as the city itself—each with its own specialty, crowd, and personality. These markets are not only places to shop but also integral to the rhythm of life in the city. Whether you're hunting for seasonal fruit, cured meats, or handcrafted goods, there's a market worth exploring nearly every day of the week.

Marché Broglie

- **Location**: Place Broglie, Strasbourg city center
- **Schedule**: Every Wednesday and Friday, 7:00 AM – 1:00 PM
- **Overview**: A quintessential French open-air market, this is a favorite among locals for fresh produce, cheeses, flowers, and prepared foods. Its central location makes it easily accessible for visitors staying downtown.

Marché de la Marne

- **Location**: Boulevard de la Marne, northeast of city center
- **Schedule**: Tuesdays and Saturdays
- **Highlights**: A large neighborhood market known for affordability and diversity, with vendors offering seasonal vegetables, free-range meats, local honeys, and even North African and Mediterranean ingredients.

Marché de Neudorf

- **Location**: Place du Marché, Neudorf district
- **Schedule**: Tuesdays and Saturdays, early morning until midday
- **Character**: Known for its bustling energy and multicultural mix, this market offers everything from Alsatian sausages to Middle Eastern pastries.

Specialty & Seasonal Markets

Christmas Markets (Marchés de Noël)

- **Location**: Various squares, especially around Place Kléber, Place Broglie, and the Cathedral
- **Dates**: Late November through December
- **Overview**: Strasbourg is widely regarded as the "Capital of Christmas," and its seasonal markets are world-renowned. Dozens of wooden chalets line the streets, offering mulled wine (vin chaud), *bredele* cookies, roasted chestnuts, *choucroute* dishes, and countless regional specialties. It's a unique opportunity to sample Alsatian comfort foods in a festive setting.

Marché Off – Strasbourg's Alternative Christmas Market

- **Location**: Place Grimmeissen
- **Vibe**: A more eco-conscious and artisanal version of the traditional holiday market. It features organic food stalls, ethical products, and vegan-friendly eats.

Marché des Producteurs

- **Location**: Rotating locations (often Place des Halles)
- **Timing**: Monthly or seasonal events featuring direct-to-consumer sales from local farms.
- **Focus**: Organic and regional foods—perfect for those looking to support small-scale Alsatian producers.

Street Food in Strasbourg

Strasbourg's street food culture has grown in recent years, reflecting both local traditions and global influences. While Alsatian fare is always within reach, the city's youthful energy has opened doors to fusion cuisine, modern takes on old recipes, and creative formats such as food trucks, night markets, and temporary food courts.

Must-Try Street Foods

- **Tarte Flambée (Flammekueche)**: This thin, crisp flatbread topped with crème fraîche, onions, and bacon is often sold from wood-fired mobile stands during festivals or markets.
- **Bretzels**: The iconic soft pretzel, often larger than your hand, served plain or with cheese, bacon, or even chocolate fillings.
- **Knack Sausage**: A Strasbourg classic—a smoked sausage with a distinct 'snap'—typically served with mustard in a baguette.
- **Crêpes & Gaufres (Waffles)**: Sweet or savory, and easy to find near the cathedral or tourist-heavy areas.

Where to Find Street Food & Food Trucks

Strasbourg Street Food Festival

- **Location**: Parc de la Citadelle or Rotating
- **Frequency**: Seasonal (usually spring/summer)

- **Description**: An eclectic mix of food trucks, pop-up kitchens, and music in an open-air setting. You'll find tacos, falafel, gourmet burgers, vegan wraps, and regional reinventions.

Les Halles – Indoor Food Court (Occasional Events)

- **Location**: Place des Halles
- **Note**: While Place des Halles is primarily a shopping center, it occasionally hosts indoor food fairs and pop-up kitchens from Strasbourg chefs and vendors.

Rue des Frères & Rue des Tonneliers

- These side streets near the cathedral have become informal street food zones, with small takeaway windows offering crêpes, doner kebabs, noodle boxes, and paninis.

Tips for Enjoying Markets and Street Food in Strasbourg

- **Bring Cash**: While many vendors now accept cards, small markets and street stalls often prefer cash, especially for low-priced items.
- **Arrive Early**: For the best selection and to avoid crowds, arrive before mid-morning—particularly at weekend markets.
- **Try Before You Buy**: Don't hesitate to ask for a taste, especially with cheeses, olives, or dried meats. Most vendors are happy to let you sample.
- **Mind the Schedule**: Many markets close around noon or early afternoon. Plan accordingly to avoid missing out.

Conclusion

Markets and street food aren't just convenient—they're immersive. They invite you into local life, encourage spontaneous culinary discovery, and celebrate the region's bounty in a way that's vibrant and accessible. Whether you're grabbing a pretzel between museums, sipping mulled wine at a winter chalet, or filling a basket with picnic supplies for the Orangerie, Strasbourg's market culture offers a satisfying taste of authenticity.

Chapter 9: Day Trips & Nearby Destinations

9.1 Colmar

Colmar is one of Alsace's most iconic towns—a jewel box of half-timbered houses, cobblestone lanes, and flower-laden canals that looks like it stepped out of a storybook. Located just over 70 kilometers south of Strasbourg, Colmar is an ideal day trip for travelers seeking to explore more of the region's charm, culture, and architectural heritage. Whether you're interested in art, wine, or just wandering picturesque streets, Colmar offers a memorable contrast to the more cosmopolitan feel of Strasbourg.

Getting to Colmar from Strasbourg

- **By Train**: The quickest and most convenient way. Direct regional TER trains run frequently from Strasbourg's central station to Colmar. The journey takes about 30 to 40 minutes, with departures nearly every half hour during peak times.
- **By Car**: Driving via the A35 motorway takes roughly 55 minutes. It's a scenic route and offers flexibility if you want to explore other villages along the way like Eguisheim or Riquewihr.

- **By Guided Tour**: Many tour operators in Strasbourg offer half- or full-day excursions to Colmar, often combining visits to multiple Alsatian villages or wineries.

What Makes Colmar Special?

Colmar blends the best of Alsace's German and French influences in a compact, easy-to-navigate layout. Its architecture is among the best-preserved in the region, and it retains a remarkably well-maintained old town that feels both vibrant and untouched by time.

You'll find everything from Gothic churches and Renaissance mansions to colorful timber-framed houses and serene canals. Colmar is often referred to as "Little Venice" due to its waterways winding through the old town—especially in the Krutenau district. Beyond the fairy-tale aesthetics, it's also a hub of Alsatian wine culture, a proud custodian of regional history, and home to the famous Isenheim Altarpiece.

Top Attractions in Colmar

Old Town (Vieux Colmar)

Wander through narrow alleyways, past painted facades and over flower-decked bridges. The old town is best explored on foot, and every corner offers something photogenic or historically significant. Highlights include the Maison Pfister, a late Gothic gem with Renaissance elements, and the Koïfhus (Old Customs House), once the economic heart of the city.

Petite Venise

This is Colmar's most famous and picturesque area. A gentle canal flanked by pastel-colored houses, Petite Venise offers postcard-worthy views and an irresistible atmosphere. Boat rides along the canal are available seasonally and provide a unique angle for photographers and romantics alike.

Unterlinden Museum

This world-class museum is housed in a former Dominican convent and is best known for the **Isenheim Altarpiece**, an awe-inspiring 16th-century polyptych by Matthias Grünewald. In addition to religious art, the museum showcases archeological finds, medieval sculptures, Renaissance paintings, and modern art.

Saint-Martin Collegiate Church

Located in the heart of the old town, this 13th-century Gothic church is one of the city's main landmarks. Its stonework and stained glass windows reflect centuries of craftsmanship and devotion.

Marché Couvert (Covered Market)

A must-visit for food lovers. This compact market hall, situated along the canal, features stalls offering local produce, cheeses, charcuterie, baked goods, and Alsatian wines. It's the perfect spot to grab a bite or pack a picnic.

Local Cuisine & Wine

Colmar is at the heart of Alsace's wine country, surrounded by some of the best vineyards on the Alsace Wine Route. Riesling, Gewürztraminer, and Pinot Gris are the regional stars. Wine tasting is readily available in town or at nearby wineries in villages like Turckheim and Ammerschwihr.

When it comes to food, traditional Alsatian dishes are abundant. Sample a hearty *baeckeoffe* (a slow-cooked meat and potato stew), crispy *tarte flambée*, or a warm slice of *kougelhopf*. Restaurants and winstubs line the town's narrow streets, offering rustic and upscale options alike.

Shopping & Artisan Goods

Colmar's boutiques and artisan shops specialize in regional crafts, textiles, Christmas ornaments (year-round in some stores), and gourmet products. If you're visiting during the holiday season, Colmar hosts one of the region's most beloved Christmas markets, with thematic chalets spread across several squares.

Don't leave without trying (or packing) some of the local delicacies such as:

- Handmade bredele cookies
- Jams made from Alsatian orchard fruits
- Foie gras terrines from family-owned producers
- Locally bottled wines in decorative Alsace flutes

Events & Seasonal Highlights

- **Spring**: Tulips and early flowers brighten the canals; crowds are minimal.
- **Summer**: Colmar's International Festival of Classical Music attracts world-class talent and lively performances throughout the town.
- **Autumn**: Harvest season means wine festivals, grape-picking excursions, and golden vineyard views.

- **Winter**: The Christmas market transforms the city into a magical wonderland, complete with glowing lights, live choirs, and warm treats.

Visitor Tips

- **Footwear**: Bring comfortable walking shoes—the old town's cobblestones can be hard on the feet.
- **Timing**: Arrive early if you're visiting during summer or December to beat the crowds and secure parking.
- **Language**: French is spoken everywhere, but many locals also speak some English and German due to the town's international appeal.
- **Photography**: Morning or golden hour brings the best light for photos, especially in Petite Venise.

Conclusion

Colmar is a feast for the senses—a town that charms with its pastel palette, enchants with its rich history, and satisfies with its culinary depth. Whether you're visiting as a quick escape from Strasbourg or building it into a longer Alsace itinerary, Colmar offers a complete cultural and visual experience that feels both intimate and grand.

9.2 Alsace Wine Route

The **Alsace Wine Route (Route des Vins d'Alsace)** is one of France's most iconic and scenic driving itineraries, stretching approximately 170 kilometers from Marlenheim (north of Strasbourg) to Thann (near Mulhouse). It winds through rolling vineyards, medieval villages, and hillside châteaux, offering a sensory journey through one of the country's most celebrated wine regions. For visitors based in Strasbourg, this route presents a perfect opportunity for a day trip or a multi-day getaway into the heart of Alsatian wine culture.

Overview of the Route

First established in 1953, the Alsace Wine Route traverses more than 70 wine-growing villages and countless family-run estates, many of which have been producing wine for generations. The landscape is defined by neat rows of vines climbing gentle hillsides, punctuated by pastel-hued houses with sloped tiled roofs and brightly colored shutters.

The region's Franco-German heritage is deeply felt in its traditions, food, architecture, and, most notably, its wine.

While the entire route can be driven in two to three days, many visitors choose to explore just a section—perhaps focusing on the area between Obernai and Ribeauvillé, or venturing farther south toward Eguisheim and Colmar.

What Makes It Unique?

Unlike France's more internationally known wine regions like Bordeaux or Burgundy, Alsace specializes almost exclusively in white wines. The region's cool, dry climate and varied soils make it particularly well-suited for aromatic varietals such as Riesling, Gewürztraminer, Pinot Blanc, Pinot Gris, and Muscat. These wines are known for their clarity, minerality, and food-friendly character.

The Alsace Wine Route isn't just about sipping wine—although there's plenty of that—it's a chance to engage directly with winemakers, walk among vines, discover hidden chapels, and enjoy the rhythm of rural French life at a relaxed pace.

Key Villages & Stops Along the Route

Obernai

Only 30 minutes from Strasbourg, this town serves as a popular starting point. It combines well-preserved ramparts, Renaissance houses, and local cellars where you can taste Riesling and Sylvaner straight from the source.

Barr & Andlau

These small towns offer a more rustic charm and access to scenic vineyards stretching up into the Vosges foothills. Andlau is particularly known for its grand cru vineyards like Kastelberg and Wiebelsberg.

Ribeauvillé

Framed by vineyard-covered hills and the ruins of three medieval castles, Ribeauvillé is both picturesque and historically rich. The town is home to some of Alsace's most respected wineries, including the well-known Trimbach estate.

Riquewihr

Often called one of the most beautiful villages in France, Riquewihr looks like a fairy tale come to life. The town itself is nearly unchanged since the 16th century and is packed with wine shops, tasting rooms, and local artisans.

Kaysersberg

Known for its colorful houses, flower-decked bridges, and charming town center, Kaysersberg also has a reputation for producing top-quality Pinot Gris and Riesling.

Eguisheim

This circular village with concentric cobbled streets is often cited as a favorite by visitors. It's the birthplace of Pope Leo IX and a stronghold for family-run wineries.

Colmar

While technically a city, Colmar can serve as a comfortable base for visiting nearby villages. Its central location makes it ideal for excursions to both the northern and southern ends of the wine route.

Wine Tasting and Visiting Estates

Most wineries along the route welcome visitors for tastings, with no pressure to purchase. While some require advance booking, especially for groups or guided tours, many smaller producers operate informal tasting rooms where walk-ins are welcome.

What to Expect:

- A warm welcome, often by the winemaker or a family member
- Tasting flights that typically include several varietals
- Options to buy directly from the cellar
- Opportunity to learn about organic or biodynamic practices, which are increasingly common in the region

Larger estates such as Maison Trimbach, Hugel & Fils, or Domaine Weinbach offer more structured tastings and may include cellar tours or guided vineyard walks.

Tip: If you're unfamiliar with Alsatian wines, don't hesitate to ask for recommendations or explanations—hosts are usually happy to guide beginners and enthusiasts alike.

Seasonal Highlights

- **Spring (April–May)**: Vineyards come to life, and the crowds are lighter. This is a great time for photographers and walkers.

- **Summer (June–August)**: Lush green vines fill the landscape, and villages host wine fairs, folk festivals, and outdoor concerts.
- **Autumn (September–October)**: Harvest season is in full swing. The foliage turns golden, and many wineries host tasting events or open-house weekends.
- **Winter (November–December)**: Villages along the route come alive with Christmas markets. The warmth of wine cellars offers a cozy contrast to the crisp air outside.

Dining Along the Wine Route

No trip through the Alsace Wine Route would be complete without savoring local cuisine. Most villages feature traditional *winstubs*—rustic wine taverns serving hearty regional dishes such as:

- **Choucroute garnie** (sauerkraut with sausages and pork)
- **Baeckeoffe** (a slow-cooked casserole of meats, potatoes, and onions)
- **Tarte flambée** (a thin crust topped with crème fraîche, onions, and lardons)
- **Munster cheese** (a strong-smelling but flavorful soft cheese, often served with cumin seeds)

Pair these with a glass of chilled Riesling or Gewürztraminer, and you have the perfect regional meal.

Transportation Tips

- **By Car**: Renting a car is the most flexible option, especially if you plan to visit more remote villages. Parking is generally free or inexpensive in most towns.
- **By Bicycle**: For active travelers, sections of the wine route are bike-friendly and dotted with marked cycling paths.
- **By Public Transport**: Limited but possible. TER trains can get you to major towns like Obernai, Colmar, and Sélestat, but local buses are sparse.
- **With a Tour Operator**: Numerous companies offer day tours from Strasbourg or Colmar with wine tastings included.

Tip: If wine tasting is your focus, consider hiring a driver or booking a tour to avoid driving under the influence.

Practical Information

- **Languages Spoken**: French is dominant, but German and English are commonly understood in tourism settings.

- **Payment**: Credit cards are accepted in most wineries and shops, though carrying a small amount of cash is wise for smaller purchases.
- **Wine Shipping**: Many wineries will arrange for international shipping if you purchase a few bottles or cases—ask about shipping options and import rules for your home country.

Conclusion

The Alsace Wine Route is more than a journey through vineyards—it's a deep dive into the soul of Alsatian heritage, where every village tells a story, and every glass of wine carries centuries of tradition. Whether you're a connoisseur or a casual traveler, this route promises a rich blend of culture, history, gastronomy, and natural beauty. From Strasbourg, it's within easy reach—and once you've experienced it, you may find yourself wanting to return, season after season.

9.3 Haut-Koenigsbourg Castle

Haut-Koenigsbourg Castle (*Château du Haut-Koenigsbourg*) stands as one of the most iconic medieval fortresses in the Alsace region. Perched dramatically on a rocky promontory at an altitude of 757 meters in the Vosges Mountains, this imposing structure overlooks the Alsatian plain, offering panoramic views that stretch on clear days to the Black Forest in Germany and even as far as the Swiss Alps. With its restored towers, drawbridges, moats, and historical displays, Haut-Koenigsbourg provides a vivid glimpse into the military, political, and feudal dynamics of the Middle Ages.

Just an hour's drive from Strasbourg, this château is a prime day trip destination for travelers looking to immerse themselves in history, architecture, and sweeping natural beauty.

Location

- **Address**: Château du Haut-Koenigsbourg, 67600 Orschwiller, France
- **Distance from Strasbourg**: Approximately 55 km (34 miles) south
- **Accessibility**: Best reached by car; also accessible via shuttle services from Sélestat during peak tourist seasons

Opening Hours

- **April to September**: 9:15 AM – 6:00 PM
- **October to March**: 9:30 AM – 5:00 PM
- **Closed**: January 1, May 1, and December 25

Note: Last entry is one hour before closing.

Admission Prices

- **Adults**: €9
- **Reduced (students, seniors, disabled)**: €5
- **Children under 6**: Free
- **Guided Tours**: Available in French and German (with printed guides available in English and other languages)

Official Website

- www.haut-koenigsbourg.fr

Key Features and Highlights

Authentic Medieval Architecture

Although a castle has existed on this site since the 12th century, much of what visitors see today was restored in the early 1900s under Kaiser Wilhelm II of Germany. The reconstruction was intended to reflect the original medieval military function and style of the fortress, making it one of the most thoroughly restored castles in France.

Defensive Design

You'll see a full range of medieval defense mechanisms: drawbridges, portcullises, bastions, and arrow slits. The architecture reflects various building techniques across the centuries, including Romanesque and Gothic influences.

Interior Exhibits

The interior features authentic furnishings, weaponry collections (swords, halberds, crossbows), and period rooms, including the lord's chambers, armory, great hall, chapel, and kitchen. Informative panels and reconstructions offer context for the castle's past inhabitants and functions.

Tower Views

Climb to the top of the keep for a commanding 360-degree view of the Alsace plain, the Black Forest, and—on clear days—the Alps. It's a photographer's dream and a favorite stop for landscape lovers.

Visitor Services

- **On-site Parking**: Free parking is available, though it can fill up quickly during holidays or weekends.
- **Shuttle Bus**: Operates between Sélestat train station and the castle during summer and school holidays.
- **Gift Shop**: Sells books, souvenirs, local crafts, and medieval-themed items.
- **Restaurant/Café**: A medieval-style tavern near the entrance offers light meals, traditional Alsatian snacks, and drinks.
- **Restrooms**: Available near the entrance and inside the castle.
- **Audio Guides & Printed Booklets**: Available in multiple languages (including English), providing historical and architectural context during your visit.

- **Accessibility**: Due to its historic structure, full wheelchair access is limited. However, many exterior paths and certain parts of the ground floor are accessible.

Tips for Visiting

- **Best Time to Visit**: Arrive early in the morning or later in the afternoon to avoid mid-day crowds, especially during summer and holidays.
- **Bring Layers**: The elevation makes it a bit cooler than the surrounding plains—bring a jacket or sweater even in summer.
- **Photographers**: Bring a wide-angle lens for interior shots and a zoom lens for panoramic vistas from the towers.
- **Educational Value**: Great for families—children often enjoy the castle's dramatic setting and interactive exhibits.

Historical Background

Originally built in the 12th century by the Hohenstaufen dynasty, the castle was destroyed during the Thirty Years' War in the 17th century and lay in ruins for over 200 years. In 1899, Kaiser Wilhelm II ordered its reconstruction to symbolize German imperial strength in Alsace, then part of the German Empire. The result is a mix of authentic medieval structure and early 20th-century historicism—making it both a legitimate castle and a statement piece of political history.

Nearby Attractions

- **Monkey Mountain (Montagne des Singes)**: A nearby wildlife park where you can walk among free-roaming Barbary macaques.
- **Eagle Park (Volerie des Aigles)**: Offers dramatic bird-of-prey demonstrations in a historic castle setting.
- **Wine Villages**: Orschwiller, Kintzheim, and Saint-Hippolyte—ideal for a wine tasting after your castle visit.

Conclusion

Haut-Koenigsbourg Castle is more than a monument—it's a portal into the feudal past of Alsace, restored with care and precision to tell the story of knights, emperors, and fortress life. Whether you're captivated by its stone towers or enthralled by its sweeping views, this site offers a rich, memorable excursion from Strasbourg. Ideal for history buffs, families, architecture enthusiasts, and photographers alike, it's one of Alsace's crown jewels—and a must-see on your journey through the region.

9.4 Black Forest (Germany)

A visit to Strasbourg places you just a short journey away from one of Germany's most enchanting regions—the **Black Forest** (*Schwarzwald*). Known for its dense evergreen forests, fairytale villages, scenic driving routes, cuckoo clocks, and soothing thermal spas, the Black Forest offers a distinctly different cultural and natural setting compared to Alsace. It's an ideal cross-border day trip that blends natural beauty, folklore, wellness, and timeless German tradition.

Whether you're seeking picturesque hikes, historic towns, hearty cuisine, or panoramic train rides, the Black Forest is packed with opportunities for exploration and relaxation—all within a one- to two-hour drive from Strasbourg.

Location and Accessibility

- **Region**: Southwest Germany, bordering the Rhine River and Alsace
- **Distance from Strasbourg**: Approximately 50–90 km (30–55 miles), depending on destination
- **Getting There**:

- **By Car**: The most flexible option—cross the Rhine into Germany via the Kehl bridge. From there, scenic routes such as the B500 (Schwarzwaldhochstraße) are easily accessible.
- **By Train**: Trains run regularly from Strasbourg to major Black Forest towns like **Offenburg, Baden-Baden, Freiburg im Breisgau**, and **Titisee-Neustadt**.
- **By Tour**: Several organized day tours depart from Strasbourg, focusing on wine tasting, Black Forest villages, or wellness retreats.

Highlights of the Black Forest

1. Baden-Baden – Spa Town Luxury

A historic Roman spa town famed for its elegant thermal baths, upscale boutiques, and neoclassical architecture. Visitors can relax in the **Friedrichsbad** or the more modern **Caracalla Spa**, both offering therapeutic hot spring waters in a serene environment. The **Lichtentaler Allee**—a leafy riverside promenade—is ideal for a peaceful stroll.

2. Triberg – Waterfalls & Cuckoo Clocks

Triberg is home to Germany's highest waterfalls and the legendary **Black Forest Museum**, which covers regional traditions, costumes, and woodcarving. The town is also the epicenter of the cuckoo clock industry, with enormous clocks and shops that are popular with tourists.

3. Titisee – Lakeside Tranquility

Located in the heart of the southern Black Forest, **Lake Titisee** is a glacial lake surrounded by thick forest and dotted with charming chalet-style hotels. Boating, swimming, and walking along the lake's edge are popular in summer, while winter brings snow sports to the surrounding slopes.

4. Schwarzwaldhochstraße (B500) – Scenic Driving Route

This legendary "Black Forest High Road" runs from Baden-Baden to Freudenstadt, offering sweeping views of the Rhine plain, alpine meadows, deep valleys, and forested ridges. There are numerous parking areas for hiking trails, photo opportunities, and forest inns offering local specialties.

5. Freiburg im Breisgau

Though technically its own day trip (see 10.4), Freiburg serves as a great gateway to the southern Black Forest. With its medieval old town, open-air markets, and sustainable urban culture, it's a worthy stop before continuing into the deeper forest.

Cultural & Culinary Experiences

Traditional Black Forest Cuisine

Expect robust, hearty dishes rooted in peasant tradition. Popular options include:

- **Schwarzwälder Schinken** (smoked Black Forest ham)
- **Bratwurst** with sauerkraut
- **Flammkuchen** (a flatbread similar to tarte flambée)
- **Venison stew** or wild boar with spätzle
- The world-famous **Black Forest Cake** (*Schwarzwälder Kirschtorte*), rich with cream, cherries, and kirsch liqueur

Artisan Craftsmanship

In villages like **Schonach** and **Furtwangen**, local artisans continue to produce traditional cuckoo clocks by hand. Visitors can tour workshops and even commission custom-made pieces. Other popular handicrafts include woodcarving, glassblowing, and traditional dressmaking.

Nature & Outdoor Activities

- **Hiking & Trekking**: Hundreds of marked trails wind through forest ridges, alpine meadows, and tranquil river valleys. Popular areas include the **Feldberg massif** and **Kaiserstuhl hills**.
- **Cycling Routes**: From mountain biking to e-bike routes through villages and vineyards.
- **Winter Sports**: In colder months, areas like **Feldberg** and **Schonach** offer skiing, snowboarding, and tobogganing.
- **Nature Parks**: The Black Forest is home to two large nature parks and Germany's first national park, **Nationalpark Schwarzwald**, which focuses on ecological preservation.

Visitor Services and Travel Tips

- **Currency**: Euro (€) – no exchange required if coming from France.
- **Language**: German is the main language, but English and French are often spoken in tourist areas.

- **Mobile Roaming**: Ensure your phone plan includes cross-border roaming, as the region straddles the German–French border.
- **Parking**: Most towns have designated lots, and roadside inns offer free or paid parking.
- **Shops Closed Sundays**: As in much of Germany, expect most stores and supermarkets to be closed on Sundays—restaurants and tourist spots remain open.
- **Weather**: Pack layers. Even in summer, weather in the forest can shift rapidly, especially at higher elevations.

Why Visit the Black Forest from Strasbourg?

The Black Forest is a striking contrast to the French Alsatian landscape—richer in alpine density, darker woodlands, and infused with Germanic folklore and culture. As a cross-border trip, it gives travelers a unique chance to enjoy two distinct regional identities in a single day. Whether you're soaking in a thermal spa, hiking through pine forests, indulging in cake and coffee at a mountain inn, or browsing a woodworker's cuckoo clock shop, the Black Forest is a refreshing change of pace that feels worlds away from urban Strasbourg—while still easily reachable.

Chapter 10: Appendix

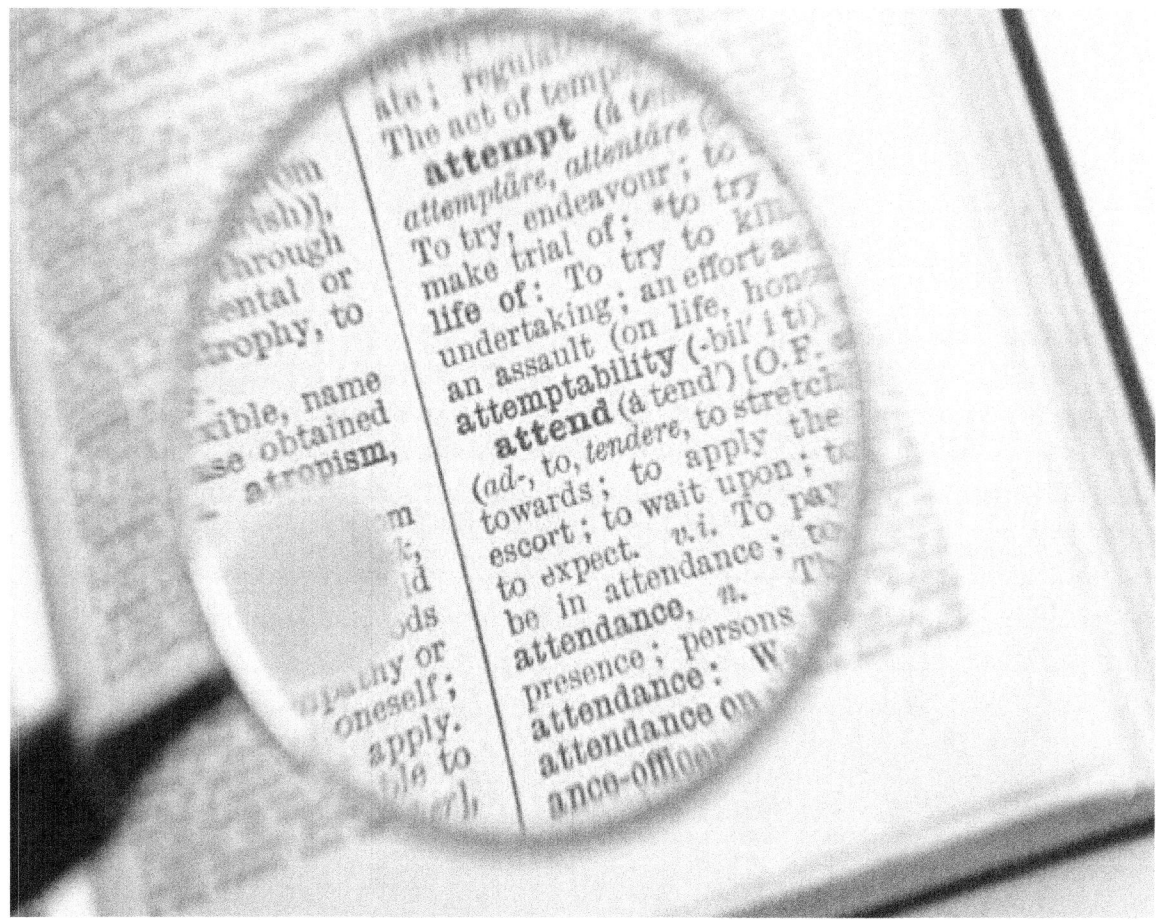

10.1 Local Emergency Contacts

When traveling to a new city—especially one in a different country—it's essential to have access to accurate and up-to-date emergency contact information. Strasbourg, being a major urban center and an international hub within the European Union, offers a well-organized emergency response system. While we all hope emergencies never arise during our travels, having these numbers at hand can be crucial in situations involving health issues, accidents, theft, or other urgent matters.

Whether you're a solo traveler, visiting with family, or coordinating a group trip, knowing whom to call—and how—is one of the most responsible steps you can take when preparing for your journey.

Important Emergency Numbers (France-wide)

The following numbers are toll-free and can be dialed from any mobile or landline phone within France, including Strasbourg:

- **General Emergency Services (SAMU – Medical): 15**
  For serious medical emergencies, including accidents, sudden illness, or when urgent care is required.
- **Police (Police Nationale): 17**
  To report crimes, theft, suspicious activity, or to request immediate police intervention.
- **Fire Brigade (Sapeurs-Pompiers): 18**
  For fires, accidents, rescues, or medical support (firefighters in France are trained first responders).
- **European Union Emergency Number: 112**
  This is a universal EU emergency number that can be dialed from any phone. The operator will direct your call to the relevant local service (medical, police, or fire). Especially useful if you're not fluent in French, as English-speaking operators are often available.
- **Poison Control Center (Centre Antipoison de Strasbourg):** +33 (0)3 88 37 37 37
  For emergencies involving toxic substances, chemical exposure, or drug overdose.

Healthcare & Medical Assistance

- **Strasbourg University Hospital (Hôpitaux Universitaires de Strasbourg)**
  Address: 1 Place de l'Hôpital, 67000 Strasbourg
  Phone: +33 (0)3 88 11 67 68 (Emergency Dept.)
  Website: www.chru-strasbourg.fr
  Strasbourg's main hospital complex, with 24/7 emergency services, multilingual staff, and specialists in all medical fields.
- **SOS Médecins Strasbourg (House-call Doctors)**
  Phone: +33 (0)3 88 75 75 75
  Website: www.sosmedecins-strasbourg.fr
  Offers 24-hour general practitioners who can make visits to hotels or accommodations when clinics are closed.
- **Pharmacies on Call (Pharmacie de Garde)**
  Pharmacies rotate overnight and holiday coverage. Call **3237** or visit www.3237.fr to find the nearest one available after hours.

Tourist Assistance Services

- **Strasbourg Tourist Office (Office de Tourisme de Strasbourg et sa Région)**
  Address: 17 Place de la Cathédrale, 67082 Strasbourg
  Phone: +33 (0)3 88 52 28 28
  Website: www.visitstrasbourg.fr
  Offers visitor assistance, maps, hotel bookings, and guidance in multiple languages.
- **Lost or Stolen Passport (U.S. Citizens)**
  - **U.S. Consulate General in Strasbourg**
    Address: 15 Avenue d'Alsace, 67082 Strasbourg
    Phone: +33 (0)3 88 35 31 04
    Website: fr.usembassy.gov
  - **Other Foreign Embassies or Consulates:**
    If your country does not have a consulate in Strasbourg, contact your embassy in Paris or the nearest EU member state embassy for emergency passport replacement or legal support.

Transport & Road Emergencies

- **Roadside Assistance (24/7 Breakdown Service)**
  - **Automobile Club Association (ACA/AA Europe):** +33 (0)3 88 76 75 75
  - **Toll Motorway Emergency (Autoroutes):** Use roadside call boxes or dial **112**.
- **Public Transport Lost & Found (CTS – Compagnie des Transports Strasbourgeois)**
  - Phone: +33 (0)3 88 77 70 70
  - Website: www.cts-strasbourg.eu

Other Useful Contacts

- **City Hall (Hôtel de Ville de Strasbourg):** +33 (0)3 68 98 50 00
  For administrative issues or in case you need to file an official report or obtain public services.
- **Local Taxis (Taxi 13 Strasbourg):** +33 (0)3 88 36 13 13
  Operating 24/7 with multiple dispatch centers across the city.
- **Electricity or Gas Emergencies (GRDF):**
  Gas Leak/Smell of Gas: 0800 47 33 33 (toll-free)
  Power Outage or Electrical Faults (Enedis): 09 72 67 50 67

Tips for Emergency Situations in Strasbourg

- **Language Help**: Emergency operators may not always speak English fluently. Learning key French phrases like *"J'ai besoin d'aide"* (I need help) or using translation apps can be useful.
- **Travel Insurance**: Always carry a copy of your insurance policy and emergency assistance hotline. Some insurers have international partnerships with local hospitals.
- **Identification**: Keep a digital and physical copy of your passport, visa (if applicable), and any important documents in a secure place and with your travel companions.
- **Stay Calm & Cooperative**: In the case of a legal or medical emergency, French authorities and healthcare professionals are generally professional, helpful, and well-trained to handle foreign travelers.

10.2 Useful French Phrases for Travelers

While many locals in Strasbourg—especially in hospitality, tourism, and younger demographics—can communicate in English, having a few French phrases under your belt can make your interactions smoother and more respectful. Even basic efforts are often appreciated and may result in more helpful or friendly responses. Whether you're ordering a meal, asking for directions, or navigating a transportation hub, the following phrases will come in handy throughout your trip.

These phrases are grouped by category to make them easier to reference while on the move.

Basic Greetings & Politeness

- Bonjour – Hello / Good morning
- Bonsoir – Good evening
- Salut – Hi (informal)
- Merci – Thank you
- Merci beaucoup – Thank you very much
- De rien – You're welcome
- S'il vous plaît – Please (formal)
- Excusez-moi – Excuse me / Sorry (formal)
- Pardon – Sorry / Excuse me (to pass)
- Au revoir – Goodbye
- À bientôt – See you soon
- Je suis désolé(e) – I'm sorry
- Oui / Non – Yes / No

Introductions & Basics

- Je m'appelle... – My name is...
- Comment vous appelez-vous ? – What's your name? (formal)
- Je suis touriste – I'm a tourist
- Je ne parle pas bien français – I don't speak French well
- Parlez-vous anglais ? – Do you speak English?
- Pouvez-vous m'aider ? – Can you help me?

Getting Around

- Où est... ? – Where is...?
- ...la gare ? – the train station?
- ...la station de tram ? – the tram station?
- ...les toilettes ? – the restrooms?
- ...un hôtel ? – a hotel?
- C'est loin ? – Is it far?
- À gauche / À droite / Tout droit – Left / Right / Straight ahead
- Combien ça coûte ? – How much does it cost?
- Je voudrais un billet pour... – I'd like a ticket to...

Dining & Food

- Une table pour deux, s'il vous plaît – A table for two, please
- La carte, s'il vous plaît – The menu, please
- Je suis allergique à... – I'm allergic to...
- Sans gluten – Gluten-free
- Sans produits laitiers – Dairy-free
- Je suis végétarien(ne) – I'm vegetarian
- L'addition, s'il vous plaît – The check, please
- C'était délicieux – It was delicious

Shopping & Markets

- Combien ça coûte ? – How much does it cost?
- Est-ce que je peux essayer ? – Can I try it on?
- Avez-vous ceci dans une autre taille ? – Do you have this in another size?
- C'est trop cher – It's too expensive
- Je paie en espèces / par carte – I'll pay in cash / by card
- Où est la caisse ? – Where is the checkout?

Emergencies & Health

- J'ai besoin d'un médecin – I need a doctor
- Appelez une ambulance – Call an ambulance
- Où est l'hôpital ? – Where is the hospital?
- Je suis perdu(e) – I'm lost
- J'ai perdu mon passeport – I've lost my passport
- Il y a eu un accident – There's been an accident
- Appelez la police – Call the police

Accommodation & Services

- Avez-vous une chambre disponible ? – Do you have a room available?
- Je voudrais réserver une chambre – I'd like to book a room
- À quelle heure est le petit déjeuner ? – What time is breakfast?
- Le Wi-Fi est-il gratuit ? – Is the Wi-Fi free?
- Où est l'ascenseur ? – Where is the elevator?
- Je voudrais annuler ma réservation – I'd like to cancel my reservation

Useful Numbers & Travel Terms

- Le tram / le bus / le taxi – The tram / bus / taxi
- Un aller simple – One-way ticket
- Un aller-retour – Round-trip ticket
- L'aéroport – The airport
- La frontière – The border
- Le passeport – Passport
- Le numéro de vol – Flight number

Pronunciation Tips

- French is largely phonetic, but pronunciation differs from English.
- Stress usually falls on the last syllable.
- Don't pronounce final consonants unless followed by a vowel (e.g., "vous" is "voo").
- Try listening to audio guides or using language apps to refine your accent.

Helpful Apps for Translation

- **Google Translate** – Offers instant text and voice translation.
- **SayHi** – Excellent for live conversations between two speakers.
- **Duolingo / Babbel** – For basic French learning before your trip.
- **Reverso Context** – Useful for understanding phrases in real-life examples.

Having a small phrasebook or saving this section on your phone can make a big difference in your travel experience. Even a simple *"Bonjour"* can open doors to warmer service and more authentic local interactions.

10.3 Public Holidays in France

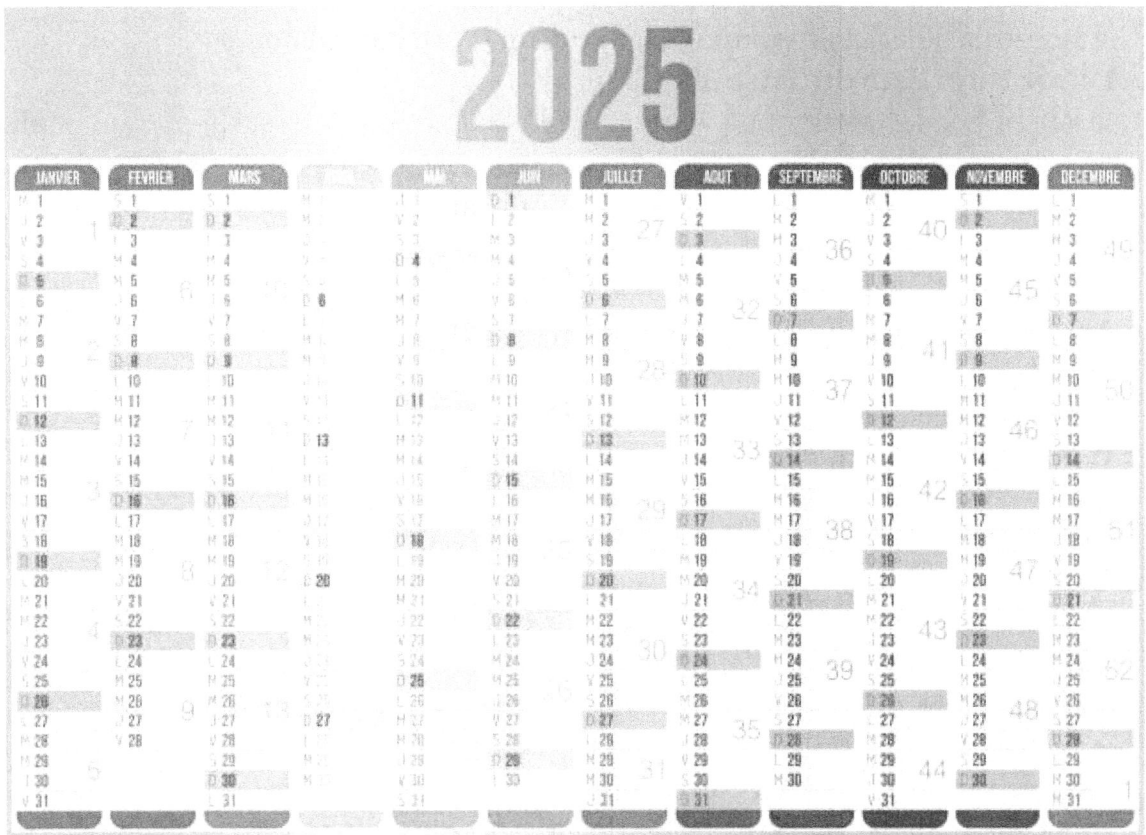

When planning your visit to Strasbourg, it's important to be aware of **France's public holidays**, as they can significantly influence your travel experience. On these days, many businesses, government offices, banks, and some attractions may be closed or operate on limited hours. Public transportation may also run on a reduced schedule. On the other hand, public holidays also offer opportunities to witness local customs, attend special events, or simply enjoy the calm rhythm of a city on pause.

Overview

France observes a total of **11 official public holidays nationwide**. In addition, some regions and cities—like Strasbourg and other parts of Alsace—observe **additional local holidays** due to historical and religious traditions unique to the region. Many of these dates are fixed, while others change each year based on the liturgical calendar.

National Public Holidays Observed in Strasbourg

1. **New Year's Day (Jour de l'An)** – *January 1*
   Marks the beginning of the new calendar year. Most places are closed, and the atmosphere is generally quiet following New Year's Eve celebrations.

2. **Easter Monday (Lundi de Pâques)** – *Date varies (March/April)*
   Celebrated the day after Easter Sunday. It's a public holiday throughout France. Many attractions and restaurants may operate with limited hours.
3. **Labor Day (Fête du Travail)** – *May 1*
   A major holiday celebrating workers' rights. Most businesses, shops, and public transport are closed. Demonstrations and parades are common in larger cities.
4. **Victory in Europe Day (Fête de la Victoire 1945)** – *May 8*
   Commemorates the end of World War II in Europe. Government ceremonies are held, and some shops or services may be closed or limited.
5. **Ascension Day (Jour de l'Ascension)** – *Date varies (40 days after Easter)*
   A religious holiday celebrated on a Thursday. It's common for people to take a "bridge holiday" (*faire le pont*) by also taking Friday off.
6. **Whit Monday (Lundi de Pentecôte)** – *Date varies (50 days after Easter)*
   Another Christian holiday observed throughout France. Originally removed as a public holiday in 2005, it has since been reinstated in many areas, including Alsace.
7. **Bastille Day (Fête Nationale)** – *July 14*
   France's national day, celebrating the storming of the Bastille in 1789. Expect parades, fireworks, and public events. It's a vibrant day in cities like Strasbourg, often filled with patriotic celebrations.
8. **Assumption of Mary (Assomption)** – *August 15*
   A major Catholic holiday celebrating the Virgin Mary's ascension to heaven. Many people take vacation around this date.
9. **All Saints' Day (La Toussaint)** – *November 1*
   A religious day to honor the dead and saints. Cemeteries are visited, and the day is generally quiet.
10. **Armistice Day (Jour d'Armistice)** – *November 11*
    Commemorates the end of World War I. Military memorial services are often held in public squares.
11. **Christmas Day (Noël)** – *December 25*
    Celebrated with family gatherings and festive meals. While Strasbourg is internationally known for its Christmas market, many shops and restaurants are closed on this day.

Additional Holidays in Alsace (Observed in Strasbourg)

Strasbourg, being part of the **Alsace-Moselle** region, observes two additional holidays that are **not recognized nationwide**:

1. **Good Friday (Vendredi Saint)** – *Date varies (Friday before Easter)*
   A regional holiday in Alsace and Moselle. Many offices and schools are closed.

2. **Saint Stephen's Day (Saint Étienne)** – *December 26*
   Celebrated the day after Christmas. Unique to this region and some European countries. Expect closures similar to Christmas Day.

Tips for Travelers During Public Holidays

- **Book Ahead:** Hotels and restaurants in Strasbourg may be fully booked during long weekends or festive periods, especially in May, August, and December.
- **Check Opening Hours:** Always verify the schedule of museums, markets, and transportation in advance. While tourist hotspots might remain open, smaller establishments often close.
- **Expect Reduced Transit Services:** Trains, trams, and buses generally operate on Sunday schedules or reduced frequency.
- **Enjoy the Celebrations:** If your visit coincides with holidays like Bastille Day or Christmas, it's a perfect time to enjoy street events, local food, and regional traditions.

Conclusion

Public holidays in Strasbourg reflect both the national identity of France and the unique cultural fabric of Alsace. By understanding these dates and their significance, travelers can plan more efficiently and take part in some of the region's most authentic moments—whether it's savoring a calm Easter Monday stroll through historic streets or watching fireworks illuminate the city on Bastille Day.

10.4 Further Reading & Resources

Whether you're planning your first visit to Strasbourg or looking to deepen your understanding of the region, having access to the right resources can make a significant difference in how smoothly and richly your trip unfolds. This section provides a curated selection of reliable sources—both online and in print—to help you explore Strasbourg and Alsace more deeply, plan your itinerary efficiently, and stay informed during your stay.

Official Tourism Resources

- **Strasbourg Tourist Office (Office de Tourisme de Strasbourg)**
  Website: https://www.visitstrasbourg.fr
  This is the official site for tourist information about Strasbourg. It offers details on current events, guided tours, opening hours for attractions, restaurant recommendations, and multilingual brochures. A must-visit resource before and during your stay.
- **Alsace Destination Tourisme**
  Website: https://www.tourisme-alsace.com
  Provides regional information beyond Strasbourg, including the Alsace Wine

Route, local traditions, seasonal events, and village highlights. Excellent for those planning day trips or a broader tour of Alsace.

- **Grand Est Regional Website**
  Website: https://www.grandest.fr
  Covers the entire Grand Est region (which includes Alsace) and features transportation updates, cultural events, and heritage sites.

Maps, Transit & Navigation Tools

- **CTS Strasbourg Transport Authority**
  Website: https://www.cts-strasbourg.eu
  Includes real-time updates on tram and bus schedules, route maps, fare information, and ticket purchasing options. Available in multiple languages.
- **SNCF (French National Railway)**
  Website: https://www.sncf.com
  Essential for booking national and international train travel. Also includes updated timetables and mobile ticketing.
- **Google Maps / Citymapper**
  These are widely used for real-time navigation, public transportation directions, and walking or cycling routes. Citymapper includes local public transit options tailored to Strasbourg.

Books for Deeper Insight

- **"Rick Steves Snapshot: Strasbourg & the Alsace"** – Rick Steves
  A user-friendly guide with practical tips for first-time visitors, including walking tours, restaurant advice, and cultural etiquette.
- **"Alsace: The Land and Its People"** – Ernest G. Black
  A more historical and cultural look at the Alsace region, including Strasbourg's unique position at the crossroads of French and German heritage.
- **"DK Eyewitness France"** – DK Publishing
  Offers detailed visuals, historical background, and itineraries, with a dedicated section on Strasbourg and Alsace.

Cultural and News Resources

- **France 24 English**
  Website: https://www.france24.com/en/
  Stay up-to-date with French news in English, including politics, culture, and travel advisories.
- **The Local France**
  Website: https://www.thelocal.fr

A useful English-language resource for news, lifestyle updates, expat information, and travel regulations.

- **Strasbourg.eu (City of Strasbourg Official Website)**
  Website: https://www.strasbourg.eu
  For updates on local policies, municipal services, safety alerts, and citywide initiatives.

Mobile Apps to Download Before You Go

- **Visit Strasbourg App**
  Available for both Android and iOS, this app includes interactive maps, self-guided tours, and a digital tourist pass with discounts to local attractions.
- **Google Translate / DeepL**
  Helpful for translating menus, signs, and casual conversations if you're not fluent in French.
- **Bonjour RATP / SNCF Connect**
  Ideal for managing national and regional transport, booking train tickets, and accessing platform information.

Academic & Historical Resources

- **JSTOR & Google Scholar**
  For academic travelers or those seeking a deeper historical perspective, you'll find peer-reviewed articles on Strasbourg's Franco-German heritage, architecture, and European Union significance.
- **UNESCO World Heritage Centre**
  Website: https://whc.unesco.org
  Strasbourg's historic city center—Grande Île—is a UNESCO site. The official UNESCO site includes criteria for its designation and historical insights.

Social Media & Travel Communities

- **Reddit: r/FranceTravel & r/Strasbourg**
  Real-time feedback, first-hand experiences, and current tips from other travelers and locals.
- **TripAdvisor Forums**
  Helpful for reading current reviews of restaurants, hotels, and tours. You can also ask specific questions and get answers from experienced visitors or local guides.
- **Instagram & YouTube Travel Channels**
  Search tags like #Strasbourg, #Alsace, or #StrasbourgChristmasMarket for up-to-date photos, food trends, and event highlights.

Final Tip

Before you finalize your travel plans, it's wise to **cross-check the most current information** from several sources, especially during busy seasons, public holidays, or in the case of local events that might affect access to certain attractions. Having a few dependable go-to resources bookmarked or downloaded can save you time and help you enjoy Strasbourg with more confidence.

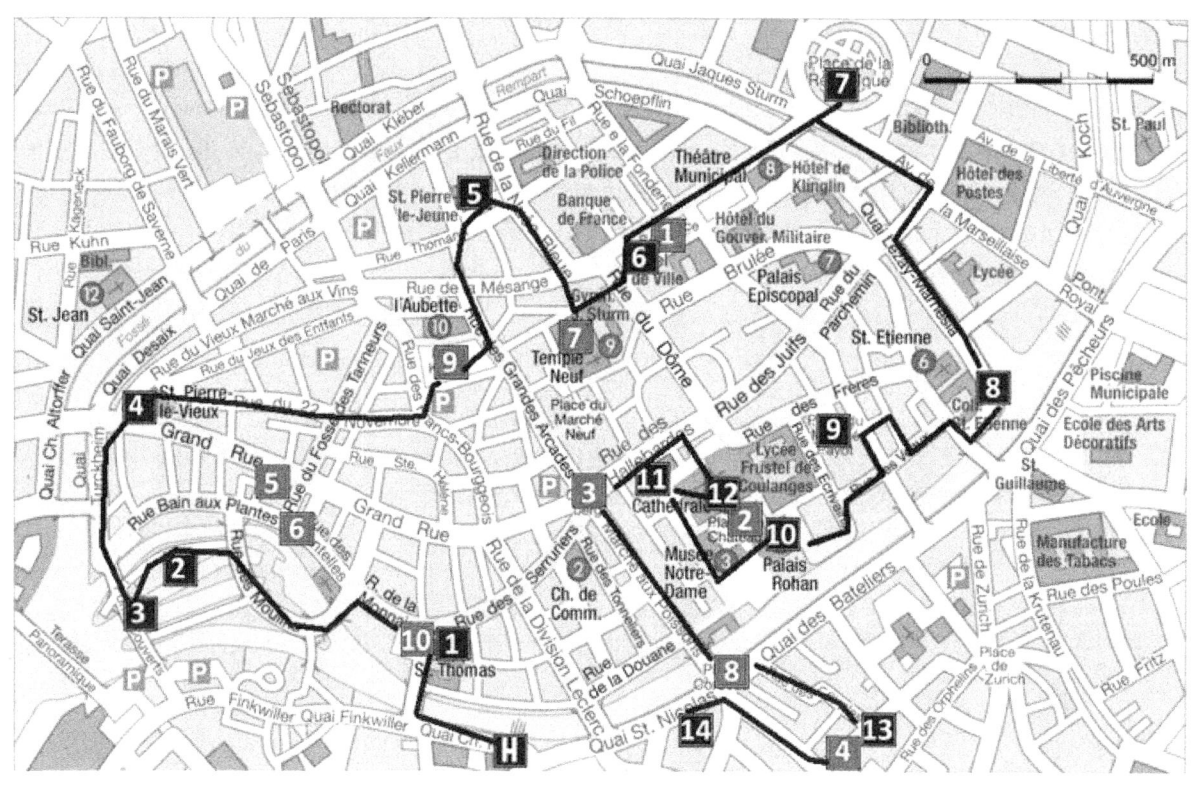

Printed in Dunstable, United Kingdom